THE INTERNATIONAL LEGAL STATUS OF FORMOSA

THE INTERNATIONAL LEGAL STATUS OF FORMOSA

by

FRANK P. MORELLO

With a foreword by

PAUL K. T. SIH

MARTINUS NIJHOFF / THE HAGUE / 1966

ISBN 978-94-015-0383-9 ISBN 978-94-015-0971-8 (eBook)
DOI 10.1007/978-94-015-0971-8

FOREWORD

Can two-Chinas co-exist in the present world order? In a sense they co-exist now—Free China in Taiwan (Formosa) and Communist China on the mainland. Barring a military showdown, this situation could remain for years to come. However, if we seek to put Free China and Communist China on some permanent basis and give them international juridical status as abiding and separate entities, then we are faced with serious difficulties. Free China and Communist China co-exist at present simply because neither can effectively alter the situation. Each is backed by a power bloc that recognizes the legal existence of only one of these political regimes. The United States does not recognize Peiping, even though it has conducted meetings on the ambassadorial level with the Regime for several years. In a corresponding way, the Soviet bloc of nations refuses to recognize Nationalist China. The situation is very similar to that of two-Germanys, two-Koreas and two-Vietnams.

To seek a solution to this political impasse, it is suggested that a "Sino-Formosan State" or some kind of "self-determination" by the Formosans be instituted. This was first expressed by Chester Bowles in his article "The China Problem Reconsidered" (*Foreign Affairs*, April 1960), and supported by John Carter Vincent in his letter to the editor of the *New York Times* (December 7, 1961). The *Conlon Report* of 1959 held the same position. Also, Arnold J. Toynbee in his article "We Must Woo Red China" (*Saturday Evening Post*, July 17, 1965) proposed that "the Taiwanese Chinese shall be allowed genuinely to determine their own destiny."

Could these suggestions lead to any solution or mean anything but wishful thinking? Before we undertake an answer it is necessary to examine fully this most complicated problem by taking all its related aspects into consideration.

Dr. Frank P. Morello, a Far Eastern political science student, earned his Ph.D. in Political Science from St. John's University, New York, in June 1965. He has devoted several years' study and research to this important issue. As a result, he is able to present this scholarly work. Considering the increasing importance of China in world affairs, this study should have a special interest for all those concerned with political developments in the Far East.

The book has several merits.

First, it has made extensive use of source materials which have not yet appeared in a similar study.

Secondly, although the author treats the problem mainly from the legal point of view, he also realizes that the issue is basically a part of the cold war and is mainly of a political nature. In this respect, he spares no effort to bring all the political elements and international considerations of the issue into proper perspective.

The third contribution that Dr. Morello makes in this work is his effort to set forth his own legal views with regard to this critical issue. He presents in a systematic way the prevailing opinions and, then, by a process of elimination, he maintains that the legal status of Taiwan should be determined by the principle of prescription.

Throughout the book, the author insists that the so-called Formosa Independent Movement is not in any sense an effective movement requiring serious consideration. His anticipation was actually confirmed by the return of Dr. Thomas Liao to Taiwan in May 1965. Dr. Liao, the head of this movement, after his return to Free China, dissolved the entire program and pledged himself to work for the unification of China in freedom under the leadership of President Chiang Kai-shek. This indicates clearly how illusory is the drive toward self-determination by the so-called Taiwanese Chinese—a solution which Arnold J. Toynbee has suggested but which Dr. Morello refutes so ably.

PAUL K. T. SIH
Director, Center of Asian Studies
St. John's University, New York

PREFACE

The scope of this work has been treated in detail in the Introduction. It becomes necessary at this point, therefore, to give a brief account of the origin and purpose of the book. The research and studies for the work were done at St. John's University as partial fulfillment of the requirements for the doctoral degree.

The work is based upon the defeat of the Kuomintang of Chiang Kai-shek by the Chinese Communists, and upon the subsequent controversy that has developed between the two governments over the sovereignty of Formosa. The question of Formosan sovereignty has been discussed by a number of nations, including Great Britain, the United States, Russia and France. In addition, the subject has been discussed by not a few writers of international law. In most instances, the complex legal questions involved in the controversy were approached from the political point of view and with political solutions in mind. The purpose of this work is to reconsider the entire question of Formosan Sovereignty from the standpoint of the legal principles of international law.

I wish to acknowledge with deepest gratitude the assistance given me by Dr. Paul K. T. Sih, Dr. Raymond L. Carol and Dr. Vincent Chen of St. John's University; and to Dr. William L. Tung of Queens College, The City University of New York all of whom contributed much in improving the book as to style, perspective and accuracy. I am also grateful to the personnel of the United Nations Library and St. John's University Library for their assistance and kind cooperation in obtaining the necessary research materials. Although I am grateful for the assistance received in this work, I alone am responsible for its contents.

FRANK P. MORELLO

New York, October, 1965

CONTENTS

I. INTRODUCTION

In recent years the question of the legal status of Formosa has become a major issue in international law and politics. Prior to 1949, the Allied Powers and the member States of the United Nations appeared to be in agreement in respect to the future status of the island. In September 1945, the Nationalist Government of Chiang Kai-shek had assumed administrative control of Formosa. Shortly thereafter, on October 25, the Nationalist Government restored the island to its former status as a province of China. At that time, neither the Allied Powers nor the United Nations objected to the apparent transfer of Formosa to Chinese sovereignty.

However, with the emergence of Communist China late in 1949, there appeared two entities claiming to represent the Chinese people and claiming rights and title to the territories of China. One of the territories under dispute was, and is, Formosa. Each entity has claimed the island as its rightful possession by virtue of the fact that it is Chinese territory. This issue is further confused because the China representation question is also unsettled. The question of the legitimate government of China has been a subject of debate in the United Nations since 1950. At the present time, it does not appear likely that either question will be settled by legal means. The reason for this apparent impasse is the strong position taken by the claimants, and the influence interjected into the issue by the United States, Great Britain, and Russia.

The Republic of China, the Central People's Republic of China, Russia, France, and India contend that Formosa is part of China. Great Britain, the United States, the Philippines, and Japan contend that the sovereignty of the island is as yet undetermined. Each country has advanced reasons in support of its position in this controversy. Some arguments appear valid, but others do not. Therefore, to place the issue in proper perspective in law, this study examines the various aspects of the problem in the light of the recognized principles of international law.

As a necessary prerequisite, the Republic of China's historical claim to Formosa must be examined. This review includes such factors as the origin of the island's early inhabitants, the first settlers, the island's first government, and the legality of China's acquisition of Formosa in 1683.

Of special interest is the cession of Formosa to Japan as a result of the Sino-Japanese war of 1894-1895. The resulting Treaty of Shimonoseki will be examined in an effort to determine Japan's legal title to Formosa as a result of the cession. Some nations ceding territory as a result of defeat in war, have considered such cessions as being made under duress. In general, the position of such nations is that the territory was stolen and that such treaties are not legally valid. The Treaty of Shimonoseki is an example of a treaty concluded under duress. In that instance, China considered Formosa as territory stolen from it by Japan. It follows then that so far as China was concerned Formosa never ceased to be an integral part of its territory. In view of Nationalist China's attitude in respect to Formosa, this study examines such treaties of cession in order to determine their validity in law.

As a victorious Allied Power, the Republic of China assumed *de facto* control over Formosa as a result of Japan's acceptance of the terms of surrender. In this instance, both claimant entities contend that Japan's acceptance of the instrument of surrender transferred title to Formosa to China. This claim by the two rivals appears to be questionable in law. Therefore, the events leading up to Japan's surrender must be reviewed. Included in this review will be the legal effect of such documents as the Cairo Declaration, the Potsdam Proclamation, the Yalta Agreement, and the instrument of surrender. In the light of these documents, the moral and legal responsibilities of the Allied Powers to "restore" Formosa to China will be examined in conjunction with an appraisal of the legal effects of these agreements on the status of the island. Each document will be examined in the light of the applicable principles of international law and placed in proper perspective to the general question of Formosan sovereignty.

Another issue which has compounded the complexity of the Formosan question is the claims of the Formosan Nationalists. This group seeks independence from China on the basis that Formosa is not Chinese territory and that Formosans are not ethnically Chinese. They consider themselves Formosans, or as they prefer to be called, "Taiwanese." The arguments presented by the Formosans are important to this study inasmuch as it now appears that there is a third group claiming title to the island. Thus, these arguments must be examined from the viewpoint of the laws of the Republic of China, as well as from the viewpoint of international law.

Basic to this study is the position taken by various states on the question of the legal status of Formosa. It is a commonly known fact that the status of Formosa continues to be a controversial issue only because such states as Great Britain, the United States, and Russia are not in agreement on the subject. An examination of the positions taken by these states indicates that their arguments are based on political factors rather than on law. An example of the political approach to the Formosan question is the "Two China" theory. This theory was proposed by some of the Allied Powers, including Great Britain and India, in an effort to settle the problem. Obviously, this question cannot be answered in simple terms. It appears that each state has been the judge in its own case and has interpreted international law to suit its specific needs or ideology.

Of primary importance to the question of Formosan sovereignty is the claim of Communist China. The Peiping regime has claimed title to Formosa based on its defeat of the Nationalist Government on the mainland of China. However, there seems to be a question about the legal status of the Peiping regime itself. This government came into existence through Russian intervention in the internal affairs of China. Furthermore, a state of war continues to exist between the two rival Chinese governments. Under these circumstances, it appears that the right of the Peiping regime to represent the Chinese people must be settled before it can claim title to Formosa.

The final subject of this examination is the claims of the Republic of China. The Nationalist Government maintains that it is the only representative of the Chinese people and denies that the question of Formosa's sovereignty exists in law. However, such states as Great Britain, Russia, France, and India do not agree with the contentions of the Nationalist Government.

The intertwining of issues and counterissues requires that each issue be examined separately within the general framework of international law. The questions involved in the legal status of Formosa are complex and controversial. However, the answers to these questions must be sought and found within the framework of international law. If it should be otherwise, the meaning of the term law as now understood among nations is reduced to absurdity.

II. EARLY HISTORY OF FORMOSA

In December 1949, Chiang Kai-shek, under the threat of the advancing Red Armies of Mao Tse-tung, transferred the seat of his government from the mainland of China to the island province of Formosa. This act by the Nationalist Government set the stage for one of the most perplexing and controversial disputes to be faced by the fledgling United Nations. The immediate issue to be settled by that organization was the China representation question. For, out of the chaos of the Nationalist defeat emerged the still unresolved problem of two governments, that of Nationalist China and that of Communist China, both claiming to represent the Chinese people. As a corollary to the China representation problem is the question of the legal status of Formosa.

The status of Formosa did not become a subject for controversy among the Allied Powers until Communist China emerged as a dominant force in Asia. Prior to that time, it was generally accepted that the island would be formally transferred to Chinese sovereignty after the conclusion of the peace treaty with Japan. However, the newly proclaimed Communist government of Mao Tse-tung, in addition to claiming to be the rightful government of China, also claimed title to all its territories, including Formosa.

Both governments have claimed title to the island on the grounds that it is an integral part of Chinese territory. This contention, however, is not shared by several member states of the United Nations, particularly Great Britain and the United States. It is the opinion of these states that the status of Formosa is as yet undetermined.

After more than fifteen years of almost continuous dispute, neither the China representation question nor the legal status of Formosa have been resolved. Such states as Great Britain, Ceylon, India, and Ireland have, from time to time, proposed solutions to the problem. However, these proposals appear to be nothing more than political solutions to a complex legal question.

In this chapter, China's historical title to Formosa is examined in order to determine the legal validity of both the Nationalist Chinese and the Communist Chinese claims. In this connection, the history of the island, its people, their culture, and language must be investigated so that the island's relationship with mainland China can be established. Furthermore, the chronology of China's original acquisition of the island, the cession of the island to Japan, and China's re-acquisition after World War II must be considered within the framework of the accepted principles of international law.

Original Inhabitants of Formosa

The island province of Formosa is located approximately 120 miles from the southeastern coast of China. The central link in a chain of islands bordering the east coast of Asia, it commands the heavily traveled sea lanes between Japan and the ports of Southeast Asia. The present population of the island is estimated to be twelve million, which is slightly more than that of Australia. Included in this population are about 210,000 aborigines. The aborigines are said to be the earliest emigrees to Formosa.[1]

The origin of the aborigines remains a matter of conjecture since Chinese historians differ as to the general area from which these people emigrated. Some Chinese scholars are of the opinion that the original emigrees were Chinese from the Northeastern section of China; their time of arrival is said to be several centuries before Christ.[2] Other scholars contend that the islands earliest inhabitants were Malayans who came from the eastern mainland of Asia.[3]

In the year 605, the Chinese navigator Ho Man arrived in Formosa and claimed the island in the name of the Sui dynasty. At that time, the island was inhabited by fierce, head-hunting aborigines with whom the Chinese could not converse.[4] The Chinese left only to return a year later with Malayan speaking natives in an attempt to establish relations with the aborigines. This effort also failed. In their chagrin, the Chinese attacked them, sacked their village, and left the island.[5]

Formosa officially became a protectorate of the Chinese empire in 1206. However, the successive dynasties maintained only a "remote and tenuous control over the island."[6]

In later years, as more immigrants arrived at the island from the

[1] "The Republic of China," Department of State, *Publication* 6844, Far Eastern Series 81, October 1959, p. 4.

[2] James William Davidson, *The Island of Formosa Past and Present*, p. 3.

[3] Seiji Hishida, "Formosa, Japan's First Colony," *Political Science Quarterly*, Vol. 22, January 1940, p. 266.

[4] Department of State *Publication* 6844, *op. cit.*, p. 6-7.

[5] Davidson, *op. cit.*, p. 3.

[6] Department of State *Publication* 6844, *op. cit.*, p. 8.

Chinese mainland, the central government appointed officials to govern them and look after their welfare.[1]

The flow of immigrants continued during the Sung and Yuan dynasties.[2] During the reign of Emperors Yung Lo (1403-1425) and Hsuen Teh (1426-1436) in the Ming dynasty, the eunuch Chengho passed through Formosa on his trips to the South Seas.[3] Not until the reign of Emperor Wan Li (1573-1620) did colonizers from the southern provinces of China begin to settle the island in large numbers and to bring the Chinese culture to Formosa.[4]

It is evident that the Chinese were the first civilized people to settle the island and establish their culture and laws there.

Early Settlers

Of special significance in establishing China's legal title to Formosa is the ethnic origin of the settlers who arrived at the island during the fifteenth and sixteenth centuries.

There were two main groups that emigrated to Formosa during this period. The first group was Japanese. This group fled Japan during the Ashikaga dynasty (1336-1443) and turned to piracy as a mode of living. Eventually, these pirate-traders established a base of operations at the port of Keelung on Formosa.

During this same period, Chinese pirate-traders occupied southern Formosa and established a base of operations in the southeastern portion of the island. The presence of both the Japanese and Chinese pirate-traders in the Formosan Straits brought about an increase in piracy along the Chinese coast. This, in turn, brought about an increase in trade among Japan, China, and the neighboring southern countries. Because of its strategic location, Formosa soon became the commercial clearing house for these nations.[5]

Most significant, however, was the continued emigration of large numbers of Chinese to Formosa from the provinces of Fukien and Kwantung. The migration of these people increased the Chinese population on the island until they greatly outnumbered the Japanese. As a result, the Chinese language, customs, and culture greatly influenced the life of Formosans.

The first Europeans to arrive in the Far East were the Portuguese

[1] *China Yearbook*, 1960-1961, p. 114.
[2] *China Yearbook*, 1957-1958, p. 56.
[3] *China Yearbook*, 1960-1961, *op. cit.*, p. 113.
[4] *China Yearbook*, 1957-1958, *op. cit.*, p. 57.
[5] Davidson, *op. cit.*, p. 7.

who appeared in Chinese waters in 1517. They were followed by the Spanish and Dutch. These three nations soon entered into an intense rivalry for the new and lucrative trade from the East. The Dutch originally moved into Java in order to dominate that area. However, early in the seventeenth century they established themselves in the Pescadores.[1] From these newly acquired bases, the Dutch harassed Spanish and Portuguese trade in the China Seas as well as the seacoast towns of China in an effort to force the Chinese into trade.

The Chinese Government, unable to cope with the formidable Dutch fleet and faced with many internal problems, entered into negotiations with the Dutch. After many months of negotiation with the authorities of Fukien province, the Dutch agreed to relinquish the Pescadores. In return, the Dutch were granted permission to settle on Formosa for commercial purposes. This transaction took place at a time when China neither exercised nor claimed any legal right to the island.[2] However, a study of the island's history up to that time reveals that the Chinese government had at least nominal rights to the island.[3] In this connection, it should also be observed that the agreement between the Fukien and Dutch authorities did not transfer title of the territory to the Dutch.

In discussing the ownership of unoccupied territory, or territory settled only by savages, Richard Zouche was of the opinion that the "ownership of such territory could be determined by conjecture."[4] Ownership is a question which neither the law nor the usages of nations has definitely settled.

In his treatment on the subject of the acquisition of unoccupied or unclaimed territory, John Basset Moore declared:

> The right of nations to countries discovered in the sixteenth century is to be determined by the law of nations as understood *at that time*, and not in the improved and more enlightened opinion of three centuries later.[5]

A similar line of reasoning can be observed in the writings of E. de Vattel. In discussing the acquisition of territory which belongs to no nation, de Vattel stated: "When a nation finds a country uninhabited and without an owner, it may lawfully take possession of it."[6]

[1] Joseph Ballantine, *Formosa, A Problem for United States Foreign Policy*, p. 5-11.
[2] Yosaburo Takekoshi, *Japanese Rule in Formosa*, (tr. by George Braithwaite), p. 55.
[3] *Cf. infra*, p. 90.
[4] Richard Zouche, *An Exposition of Fecial Law and Procedures*, Vol. 2, (tr. by J. L. Brierly and ed. by James Brown Scott), p. 76-77.
[5] John Basset Moore, *A Digest of International Law*, p. 259.
[6] E. de Vattel, *The Law of Nations or the Principles of International Law*, (tr. of the edition of 1758 by Charles G. Fenwick)p. 84.

If this line of argument is acceptable, it is quite possible that the Fukien authorities had the legal right to grant the Dutch permission to settle on the island.[1] Therefore, the agreement appears to be in accordance with the principles of international law as understood and practiced at that time.

Upon settling in Formosa, the Dutch lost little time in consolidating their position. They built the forts of Providentia and Zeelandia. Shortly thereafter, the Dutch imposed so many trade restrictions on the Chinese and Japanese inhabitants that the antagonism between the Dutch and the natives became intolerable. The Japanese finally left Formosa during the second quarter of the seventeenth century.[2] Despite the Dutch treatment, however, the Chinese remained and further expanded both their territorial holdings and population.

Kingdom of Koxinga

The increase in the Chinese population on Formosa was due to the continual unrest and chaos existing on the mainland during the latter part of the seventeenth century. During this period China underwent a civil war as well as a Tartar invasion. As a result, many mainlanders emigrated to Formosa.

Out of this period emerged one of the most extraordinary men of Chinese history, Cheng Ch'eng-Kung, better known to Westerners as Koxinga. Because of his exploits, Formosa eventually became an integral part of China. No study of the political history of the island would be complete without his story.[3]

Koxinga was the son of Cheng Chi-lung, a powerful pirate-trader who aligned himself with the Ming dynasty in the great struggle between the Ming and Manchu dynasties. Cheng was eventually captured and imprisoned by the Manchus. Young Koxinga took his father's place and carried on the fight to restore the Ming dynasty.

After engaging the Manchus in many battles, Koxinga was forced to retreat to the island of Amoy. Eventually, he established a base in the Pescadores and from that vantage point he inflicted much damage on the Manchu forces. While in the Pescadores, Koxinga decided to take Formosa from the Dutch and establish his headquarters on the island.

In 1661, he assembled an army of 25,000 men and an armada of war

[1] *Cf. supra.* According to James Davidson, the island was formally ceded to the Dutch in 1623.

[2] Takekoshi, *op. cit.*, p. 58-59.

[3] Maclear Bate, *Report From Formosa*, p. 31-32.

junks, and set sail for Formosa. He landed his troops near Fort Zeelandia and engaged the Dutch in battle at both forts. Fort Providentia was quickly taken. However, the Dutch at Fort Zeelandia offered stronger resistance and it was not until October 1662 that the Dutch finally surrendered. With the end of Dutch resistance, came the end of 30 years of Dutch rule in Formosa.[1]

Two significant factors contributed to the easy defeat of the Dutch by Koxinga. The first was the ineffectiveness of Dutch authority and control on Formosa. They had little or no control over the aborigines, and their control over the Chinese population was loose and of an administrative nature. The strong points of Dutch military control appear to have been in the areas of Forts Zeelandia and Providentia and at some of the port areas. This lack of effective control by the Dutch left the island vulnerable to the seaborne attacks of Koxinga's forces and the eventual defeat of the Dutch forces on the ground.[2]

The second factor in Koxinga's campaign against the Dutch was the role played by the island's Chinese population. These people effectively supported Koxinga and helped bring about the Dutch defeat. The descendants of these people and the earlier Chinese pirate-traders now consider themselves Formosan Nationalists and are conducting a campaign for independence from Chinese Nationalist rule.[3]

After the defeat of the Dutch, Koxinga established himself as the island's sovereign. He introduced Chinese laws, customs, and forms of government. In this manner, he obliterated all traces of former Dutch rule and institutions.

In establishing his kingdom, Koxinga did not consider Formosa as separate from the Chinese Empire. His ambition was to depose the ruling Manchu dynasty in favor of the ousted Mings. However, he was not to realize his ambition as he died at the age of 39.

Koxinga was succeeded to the throne by his son Cheng Ching who, like his father, refused to accept the Manchu court. Cheng Ching died in 1682, and the throne was assumed by his 12 year-old son, Cheng Koshwang. The boy king was no match for the Manchu forces. In July of 1683, the island was surrendered to the government at Peking. The surrender ended the rule of the Koxingas, and Formosa was absorbed into the Chinese Empire.[4]

[1] Takekoshi, *op. cit.*, p. 63-64.
[2] Davidson, *op. cit.*, p. 31-47.
[3] Kleinwatcher, "The History of Formosa Under Chinese Nationalist Government," *China Review*, Vol. 12, 1884, p. 386.
[4] Ballantine, *op. cit.*, p. 13-16.

Legality of China's Acquisition of Formosa

October 1683 may be accepted as the date when Formosa became a Chinese possession. So far as is known, the acquisition of Formosa by China was in accordance with the principles of international law as understood and practiced at that time.

According to the rules of international law, the transfer of sovereignty from one state to another can be effected by treaty, annexation, cession, subjugation, or accretion. In addition, title can also be acquired by *de facto* occupation of territory, provided the occupation remains in effect over a long period of time. However, a necessary condition of occupation is that the territory is not claimed by another state or does not already form a part of the dominions of any state.[1]

At the time of its acquisition by the Manchu dynasty, Formosa was not claimed by a third state, nor did it form a part of the territory of another state. The island was an independent kingdom governed by a Chinese subject who was hostile to the reigning dynasty. Eventually, the Manchus prevailed and the island was surrendered to China. The surrender, though peaceful, constituted a conquest by the Manchus. Since there is no evidence available that a treaty of cession was effected between the two governments, it appears that the most logical mode by which China acquired title to the island was by subjugation. In discussing subjugation, Professor Oppenheim declared:

> Conquered enemy territory, although actually in the possession and under the sway of the conqueror, remains legally under the sovereignty of the enemy until through annexation it comes under the sovereignty of the conqueror. Annexation turns the conquest into subjugation.[2]

The opinions of earlier writers on international law do not vary greatly from those of Oppenheim. In his discourse on conquest, Alberico Gentili said: "Therefore, to mulct the conquered in land was usual with the Romans and was just. ... So, too, tributes and acquisition are according to the law of God."[3]

Hugo Grotius, though agreeing that occupied territory belongs to the conqueror, sets forth the conditions of a time limit and the ability of the conqueror to maintain his hold on the territory. In his discussion on "the Rights of Acquiring Things Taken in War," he states:

[1] James Brierly, *The Law of Nations*, p. 151.
[2] Laurence Oppenheim, *International Law, A Treatise*, Vol. 1, (ed. by Hersch Lauterpacht), p. 567.
[3] Alberico Gentili, *De Jure Belli Libri Tres*, Vol. 2, p. 304.

Only that territory will be regarded as captured which is so surrounded by permanent fortifications that the other party will have no access to it openly unless these have first been taken.[1]

On the other hand, Samuel Pufendorf does not agree that the conqueror has a legal right to conquered territory unless a treaty of cession is effected. According to Pufendorf, annexation or force cessions are not valid agreements. In discussing the subject Pufendorf stated: "For alienation means, first and foremost, that a thing passes from a willing owner, and that it is not taken from him against his will by mere violence."[2]

Thus, Koxinga and his descendents were considered enemies of China by the Manchus. Under these circumstances, the transfer of the island to Chinese sovereignty was in the nature of a conquest which was later followed by annexation. It is evident that if the arguments of Grotius, Gentili, and Oppenheim are accepted, the acquisition of Formosa by China was in accordance with the principles of international law as understood and practiced by nations during that time.

Formosa under Chinese Rule

Chinese administration of the island was loose and rather ineffective from the very beginning. The successful administration of the island by the Manchu dynasty was foiled by the following factors: (1) the geographical separation between the island from the mainland, (2) weak and corrupt Manchu administrators, (3) the existence of dissident elements still loyal to the Ming dynasty, and (4) the administration's inability to control the wild tribes inhabiting the eastern and southern portions of the island.

The inability of the Manchu administrators to maintain order resulted in widespread lawlessness and banditry. The aborigines, in particular, imprisoned and murdered many American, European, and Japanese seamen who had the misfortune of being shipwrecked on the island. Most of the nations whose seamen were murdered or maltreated protested to the Chinese Government. However, the Chinese disclaimed responsibility for the atrocities committed by the aborigines in territory not under its control.[3]

In one such incident, 50 Japanese sailors were murdered by the Botan tribesmen in the southern portion of the island. The Japanese

[1] Hugo Grotius, *De Jure Belli Ac Pacis Libri Tres*, Vol. 2, p. 667.
[2] Samuel Pufendorf, *De Jure Naturae et Gentium, Liber Octo*, (tr. by C. H. Oldfather and W. A. Oldfather), p. 606-612.
[3] Owen Rutter, *Through Formosa, An Account of Japan's Island Colony*, p. 36.

Government protested to the Chinese authorities but their protests were met with indifference by the Chinese Government. As a result, the Japanese launched an expedition in April 1874 to punish the offending tribesmen.

In the beginning, the Chinese Government did not object to the Japanese action. However, it later reversed its position and declared all Formosa under the jurisdiction of China. The Japanese action was significant for two reasons. First, the expedition led to effective control over the tribesmen by the Chinese authorities.[1] Second, the Japanese renewed their ambition to take eventual possession of the island.

Japanese Acquisition of Formosa

The Japanese had long desired to make Formosa a part of its colonial empire. Its first attempt to seize the island occurred in the sixteenth century during the Tokugawa Dynasty. At that time, Japanese pirate-traders were using a portion of the island as a base of operations. In the beginning the Japanese Government had been content to share the island with the Chinese. However, in 1615, when the Western nations became active in the China seas, the Japanese attempted to annex Formosa by force. A force of 3000 men led by Murayama, the governor of Nagasaki, landed on the island. The invasion was short-lived, however, as the Chinese, aided by the local population, easily defeated the Japanese.[2]

In the third quarter of the nineteenth century, after it had emerged from its long self-imposed seclusion, Japan again sought to acquire Formosa. The opportunity finally arrived in July 1894 when war broke out between the two countries. The Japanese forces easily defeated the Chinese and, on April 12, 1895, the Treaty of Shimonoseki terminated the Sino-Japanese War. The treaty provided for the cession of Formosa and the Pescadores to Japan. The Chinese Government had no intention of relinquishing sovereignty of the island and strongly opposed the Japanese demands. The Japanese would not agree to a peace unless Formosa was transferred to its sovereignty. Finally, the Chinese yielded and the treaty was ratified by both governments on May 8, 1895.[3]

Formal transfer of the island to Japan took place on June 2, 1895. In commenting on the transfer, Yosaburo Takekoshi, a Japanese official, expressed the sentiments of his government when he said:

[1] Ballantine, *op. cit.*, p. 19.
[2] Davidson, *op. cit.*, p. 7.
[3] Ballantine, *op. cit.*, p. 23.

and thus, the island which China had torn from Koxinga's descendants by intrigue, bribery and brute force, passed again into the hands of the Japanese in whose veins flow the same blood as filled those of Koxinga.[1]

It is evident from Takekoshi's statement that the Japanese government based its claims to Formosa on the fact that Koxinga was part Japanese. The Chinese government, however, never placed much importance on this fact and considered Koxinga and his descendants as Chinese. China also based its claims to Formosa on the fact that the island's earliest settlers were Chinese and that it had possessed the territory since 1683. During the 50 years of Japanese rule, the Chinese government considered Formosa as a part of its territory temporarily separated from it.

The island became a subject of international concern during World War II. During that time, several conferences were held by the Allied Powers which resulted in an agreement concerning the future status of the island and other former Chinese territories then in the possession of Japan. These conferences and their effect on the status of Formosa are very important in the light of the present situation in China.

[1] Takekoshi, *op. cit.*, p. 86.

III. CONFERENCES AND DECLARATIONS: THEIR EFFECT ON THE STATUS OF FORMOSA

Between 1894 and 1942, China lost a considerable amount of its territory to Japan as a result of the latter's expansionist policies. Among the territories lost was the island of Formosa. Although it was ceded to Japan in accordance with the terms of the Treaty of Shimonoseki, the Chinese Government had considered the island as territory wrested from it under duress. Following this line of argument, the Chinese considered the island as stolen territory and, therefore, as never having left Chinese sovereignty. The argument of the Chinese Government does not appear to be valid in this instance.[1] In this connection, international lawyers such as Fenwick[2] and Hyde[3] are agreed that the enforced cession of territory confers a valid legal title to the recipient. However, these authorities also agree that there is a moral objection to the recognition of title to a territory acquired in such a manner.[4] In discussing treaties of cession concluded under duress, Brierly declared:

> that the latter (enforced cession) has in the past conferred a valid legal title is undeniable... So long as war continues to be used as an instrument of national policy, it will continue to produce the same results as it has in the past, and one of those results will be the annexation of territory.[5]

It is evident that cessions made as a result of a treaty of peace are valid in law. The fact that the ceding state does not agree to the cession on moral grounds does not have any effect on the formal transfer of its territory to the victorious state. The claim by the Nationalist Chinese that enforced cessions are not legal appears to be questionable.

Cairo Conference

The Cairo Declaration of 1943 eventually became the basis for future

[1] Claude S. Phillips, Jr., "The International Legal Status of Formosa," *Western Political Quarterly*, Vol. 10, 1957, p. 282.
[2] Charles G. Fenwick, *International Law*, p. 360.
[3] Charles Cheney Hyde, *International Law, Chiefly as Interpreted and Applied by the United States*, Vol. 1, p. 359.
[4] Chen Ti-chiang, *The International Law of Recognition*, p. 430.
[5] James L. Brierly, *The Law of Nations, An Introduction to the International Law of Peace*, p. 155-156.

Allied policy toward Formosa. At the time of the conference, neither Chiang Kai-shek nor the Allied Powers could foresee the coming struggle between the Nationalists and the Communists for control of the Chinese mainland. Therefore, no legal questions about the transfer of sovereignty from Japan to the Republic of China were raised by any of the Powers. It was the Allied intention that the Nationalist Government would occupy the island and assume administrative control until a treaty of peace was effected with Japan. At that time, it was assumed that Formosa would be formally retroceded to the Republic of China. However, the subsequent loss of the mainland to the Chinese Communists and the establishment of the seat of the Nationalist Government on Formosa have changed the situation completely. What at first appeared to be a simple solution to a minor problem has now become one of the most complex international problems of our time.

The groundwork for the return of Formosa to the Republic of China was laid at the Roosevelt-Chiang meeting on November 23, 1943 at President Roosevelt's villa in Cairo. During this meeting, President Roosevelt agreed with Chiang Kai-shek that Formosa should be restored to China. There has been no official American record issued or published concerning the substance or results of the meeting between the two Heads of State. However, a summary record in the Chinese language was found in the files of the Nationalist Government. The editors of the "Foreign Relations of the United States" made a request to the Nationalist Government that an English translation of the conversation be prepared, and that they be given permission to publish its contents. The Nationalist Government agreed to their request. The translation of the Chinese summary record is as follows:

> Generalissimo Chiang and President Roosevelt agreed that the Four Northeastern provinces of China, Taiwan (Formosa), and the Penghu Islands (Pescadores) which Japan had taken from China by force must be restored to China after the war.[1]

Further evidence that President Roosevelt committed the United States to the eventual return of Formosa to the Republic of China appears in Roosevelt's papers. In the "Minutes of a Meeting of the Pacific War Council" at Washington on January 12, 1944, President Roosevelt informed the Council that:

[1] United States, Department of State, "The Conference at Cairo and Teheran," *Foreign Relations of the United States*, 1961, p. 324.

his discussions with Generalissimo Chiang Kai-shek and with Marshal Stalin were highly satisfactory, in that both agreed that Japan should be stripped of her island possessions... Marshal Stalin had specifically agreed that Manchuria, Formosa, and the Pescadores should be returned to China.[1]

It should be observed that Stalin's statement in connection with the restoration of Formosa to China was made in the confidence of the conference table. A public acceptance of the Cairo Declaration by Russia would have been considered a hostile action by Japan and would have resulted in war between the two countries.

As a result of the first Cairo Conference held during November 22-26, 1943, a press communique was released at Cairo on November 26, 1943. The communique read in part:

It is their (The United States, China and Great Britain) purpose that Japan be stripped of all the islands in the Pacific which she has seized or occupied since the beginning of the First World War in 1914, and has stolen from the Chinese, such as... Formosa... shall be restored to the Republic of China.[2]

The Cairo Declaration was the first joint declaration by the United States, Great Britain, and China in respect to the future status of Formosa. With the exception of Russia, the Allied Powers had agreed to restore the island to the Republic of China. That a commitment was made to China by her Allies is unquestioned. However, the legal binding effects of the Cairo Declaration has become a subject of controversy among the Allied Powers in recent years. The binding effects of this and other commitments, particularly on Russia, will be discussed subsequently.

Because Russia was not at war with Japan at the time of the Cairo Conference, Marshal Stalin did not participate in its first phase. As a result, Russia was not a signatory to the Declaration of November 26, 1943. However, during a discussion with President Roosevelt and Prime Minister Churchill at the time of the Teheran Conference, Marshal Stalin concurred with the substance of the Cairo Declaration. The results of the meeting among the three Heads of State has been recorded in the "Bohlen Minutes" of the Teheran Conference. Mr. Bohlen's Minutes read in part:

For the next part of the luncheon the conversation was general, until the Prime Minister asked Marshal Stalin whether he had read the proposed communique on the Far East of the Cairo Conference.

[1] *Ibid.*, p. 568-569.
[2] *Ibid.*, p. 448.

Marshal Stalin replied that he had and although he could make no commitments he thoroughly approved the communique and all its contents. He said that it was right that ... Formosa and the Pescadores Islands should be returned to China.[1]

This statement by Marshal Stalin is the first open indication of the Russian attitude toward the future status of Formosa. Wishing to maintain an atmosphere of cooperation with its Allies, Russia agreed in principle to the substance of the Cairo Declaration. However, Russia was not bound to the Declaration since it was not a signatory to that pact.

Potsdam Conference

The United States, apprehensive of Russian intentions toward China after the war, proposed to strengthen its policy in the Far East by obtaining Soviet adherence to the Cairo Declaration. In this connection, the President and his advisors were of the opinion that:

a commitment by the Soviet Union to adhere to the Cairo Declaration would need to be supplemented by a detailed understanding as to the course of action to be taken in the Far East and Pacific by the Governments of the Soviet Union and the United States. Such an understanding would appear to be necessary to guard against Soviet attempts to set up friendly governments in... China as a whole.[2]

As a result of the American Government's efforts to obtain Soviet acceptance of the Cairo Declaration, its terms were reiterated in the Potsdam Proclamation. The Proclamation, issued on July 26, 1945, and approved by the Heads of Government of the United States, China and Great Britain, called for the surrender of Japan. Paragraph (8) of the Proclamation specified that: "The terms of the Cairo Declaration shall be carried out."[3]

Contrary to American expectations the Soviet Government did not become a signatory to the Potsdam Proclamation. In justifying his actions, Stalin claimed that Russia was still at peace with Japan. Furthermore, the Soviet leader was reluctant to commit himself until the Allies agreed to his demands and until Russia had settled its problems with China.[4] However, when the Allied victory over Japan

[1] *Ibid.*, p. 565-568.

[2] United States Department of State, "The Conference of Berlin (Potsdam)," *Foreign Relations of the United States*, 1960, p. 927.

[3] *Ibid.*, p. 1475.

[4] United States Department of State, "Argument Regarding Entry of the Soviet Union Into the War Against Japan," *Foreign Relations of the United States, Diplomatic Papers*, Publication 6199, 1955, p. 984.

appeared imminent, Russia declared war on that nation. In a statement handed to the Japanese Ambassador and published in the Soviet Press on August 8, 1945, Foreign Minister Molotov declared:

Taking into consideration the refusal of Japan to surrender, the Allies approached the Soviet Government with a proposal to join the war against Japanese aggression... Faithful to its obligations to its Allies, the Soviet Government accepted the proposal of the Allies and adhere to the statement of the Allied Powers of July 26, 1945... As of 9 August, the Soviet Union will consider it is in a state of war with Japan.[1]

That, declaring war against Japan, the Soviet Union also agreed to adhere to the terms of the Cairo Declaration is a matter of history. Most significant is the fact that the remaining Allied Powers have not yet agreed to the restoration of Formosa to the Republic of China.

Instrument of Surrender

The Instrument of Surrender reiterated the provisions of the Cairo Declaration and the Potsdam Proclamation. Signed and accepted on September 2, 1945, by the representatives of Japan and the Allied Powers, its provisions stated in part:

The Japanese Government and the Japanese Imperial General Headquarters, hereby accept the provisions set forth in the declaration issued by the Heads of Government of the United States, China, and Great Britain on July 26, 1945, at Potsdam.[2]

Although the surrender document did not specifically refer to Formosa, it unquestionably stipulated complete acceptance of and compliance with the provisions of the Potsdam Proclamation. Accordingly, the Japanese forces on the island surrendered to the Nationalist Government which assumed immediate administrative control of the organs of government. Although Japan did not formally transfer title of Formosa to China, it no longer exercised any control over the territory.

The Effect of the Cairo and Potsdam Declarations and the Instrument of Surrender on the Status of Formosa

The legal effect of declarations such as Cairo and Potsdam relative to the status of Formosa appears to be questionable. However, the spokesmen for the Republic of China contend that the Cairo Declara-

[1] "The Conference of Berlin (Potsdam)," *op. cit.*, p. 1474.

[2] United States Department of State, *Division of Research and Publication*, Bulletin No. 324, Publication No. 2384, Vol. 13, 1945, p. 364.

tion and the Potsdam Proclamation are "legal and binding upon the signatories."[1] Furthermore, the Republic of China contends that these documents became binding on Japan at the time of its acceptance of the terms of surrender on September 2, 1945. The views of the Nationalist Government are not shared by all international lawyers. In his treatment on declarations, Oppenheim is of the opinion that the Cairo and Potsdam documents were official statements in the form of reports and conferences signed by the Heads of States which could be regarded as legally binding on the signatories. However, he declared that:

> Declarations of this kind may be very important but they hardly comprise transactions out of which follow rights and duties of other states.[2]

If this line of argument is to be accepted, the Chinese Nationalist claim that title to Formosa passed to China after the surrender of Japan appears to be questionable. The Republic of China, however, is adamant in its opinion that title to Formosa has passed to China and the island is an integral part of Chinese territory. In support of his Government's position on the subject, President Chiang Kai-shek declared:

> Therefore, when Japan surrendered, the Government of the Republic of China repossessed Taiwan (Formosa) and Penghu (Pescadores) and constituted them as Taiwan Province. Since that time, Taiwan and Penghu have regained their status as an integral unit of the territory of the Republic of China.[3]

The Nationalist Government's claim in this instance is based on the assumption that Japan's acceptance of the Potsdam Proclamation has, in effect, transferred title of the island from Japan to China. From the Chinese point of view, the acceptance of the surrender terms are interpreted as a surrender of Japanese sovereignty. The Chinese viewpoint is not shared by the Allied Powers nor is it shared by some international laywers. In his treatment of the subject Professor D. P. O'Connell declared:

> Neither the Potsdam Proclamation nor the instrument of surrender appear to have transferred sovereignty of the territory to China... the legal effect of the Japanese acceptance of the surrender is by no means clear.[4]

[1] Republic of China, "News Conference of October 16, 1959," *Ministry of Foreign Affairs*, p. 1.

[2] Laurence Oppenheim, *International Law, A Treatise*, Vol. 1 (ed. by H. Lauterpacht), p. 872-873.

[3] Chiang Kai-shek, "President Chiang Reviews World Situation," *China News Service*, February 1955, p. 3.

[4] Donald O'Connell, "Legal Aspects of the Peace Treaty with Japan," *The British Year Book of International Law*, (ed. by E. Lauterpacht), 1953, p. 425.

Thus, it appears that the claims of the Nationalist Government concerning the transfer of the sovereignty of Formosa are open to discussion. The Cairo Declaration was, at best, a statement of purpose among the Allied Powers. How far the parties to that Declaration are legally bound to carry out its provisions is questionable.

Furthermore, the Japanese acceptance of the Instrument of Surrender, through it relieved Japan of *de facto* control of Formosa, did not transfer title of the territory to China. Sovereignty in law remained with Japan until it formally renounced title to the island in 1952. The Japanese renunciation has further complicated the issue. In addition to the claims of Communist China, the position of the Nationalist Government has also been challenged by the Formosan Nationalists.

IV. CLAIMS OF THE FORMOSAN NATIONALISTS

A study on the legal status of Formosa would be incomplete without examining the views and claims of the Formosan Nationalists. The Formosans, also referred to as the Taiwanese, have sought complete separation from both Chinas. It is their contention that they owe allegiance neither to the Nationalist Government nor to the Peiping regime of Mao Tse-tung.

The Formosan claims to the island's sovereignty are based on several assumptions. First, they claim that the Cairo Declaration is not valid, as it violates the terms of the Atlantic Charter. The basis for the violation is the fact that the Declaration handed Formosa to China without the consent of the Formosan people.[1] Second, the Formosans agree with Great Britain and India that the island is not a part of Chinese territory and, therefore, they have the right to self-determination.[2] Third, the predominantly Chinese ethnic origin of the population does not necessarily make them Chinese. Finally, long political separation from China and misrule by the Chinese authorities have given the Formosans the right to independence.[3]

Following this line of argument, the Formosans have voiced a desire for complete independence and admission to the United Nations as a new state. In the event that independence is not possible, the Formosans then desire to be placed under a United Nations trusteeship until such time as the legal status of the island has been determined. It is of special interest to this study, therefore, that the validity of the Formosan claims be examined and evaluated. Moreover, it is important that these arguments be placed in their proper perspective relative to the general question of Formosan sovereignty.

The arguments advanced by the Formosan Nationalists cannot be construed as to represent the views of all Formosans. It is quite possible that this group represents a minority rather than a majority of native Formosans.[4]

[1] Li Thian-hok, "The China Impasse," *Foreign Affairs*, Vol. 36, April 1958, p. 447.
[2] Joshua Liao, *Formosa Speaks*, p. 52-53.
[3] Li Thian-hok, *op. cit.*, p. 444-445.
[4] After the Article, "The China Impasse," by Li Thian-hok was published in *Foreign Affairs*, the late Mr. Alfred Kolberg wrote to Mr. Hamilton F. Armstrong, editor of

Chinese Law on Nationality

The historical and ethnical background of the population of Formosa was established in Chapter II. With the exception of the aborigines, there is little question that the population of Formosa is of predominantly Chinese stock. Furthermore, except for the 50 years of Japanese rule, the customs, laws, language, and economy of the island have been essentially Chinese.[1]

The Formosan claim that they are not essentially Chinese appears questionable when examined from the standpoint of Chinese history and law. The official Chinese policy on nationality has always been that persons born of Chinese parents, no matter where they happen to reside, are nationals of China.[2]

In his treatment on the subject of nationality, Professor Schwarzenberger declared:

> It has been the practice of states to exercise territorial jurisdiction over all persons within their territory because of the presence therein of such individuals, and personal jurisdiction over their nationals on the ground of the allegiance they owe, wherever they happen to be.[3]

In accordance with the principles of international law, nationality may be acquired by birth or by naturalization. In acquiring nationality by birth, a person must be either born in the territory of a state or be born of a person having the nationality of the state. These are the principles of *jus soli*, the territorial principle, and the principal of *jus sanguinis*, the blood-relation principle. Therefore, according to Professor Von Schuschnigg:

> a State may not confer its nationality at birth upon a person except on the basis of (a) a birth of such person within its territory or a place assimilated thereto (*jus soli*), or (b) the descent of such persons from one of its nationals (*jus san guinis*).[4]

It is evident from the preceding analysis that the Formosans are Chinese, both in origin and in law. Formosan attempts to disassociate themselves from their ethnic origin are neither logical nor valid.

Foreign Affairs seeking Li's identification. Mr. Armstrong replied that Li Thian-hok is the pen name of the author whose identification could not be revealed. Until the author's identification is established, the article can be considered only as an academic study and not as something which would represent the real feeling or opinion of the people of Formosan origin, since the author could be either Formosan or not.

[1] James William Davidson, *The Island of Formosa, Past and Present.* p. 2-3.

[2] For details see William L. Tung, *China and Some Phases of International Law*, chapter IV; for the text of the Chinese Nationality Law, see same author, *Cases and Other Readings on International Law*, Shanghai, 1940, p. 134, 142-43, 148-49.

[3] Georg Schwarzenberger, *A Manual of International Law*, Vol. 1, p. 129.

[4] Kurt Von Schuschnigg, *International Law, Introduction to the Law of Peace*, p. 191

Republic of Formosa

In support of their argument for independence, the Formosans contend that the Treaty of Shimonoseki, which ceded Formosa to Japan was not legal since the cession was not in accordance with the wishes of its inhabitants.[1]

The majority of Formosans were opposed to the cession. Therefore, in an attempt to prevent the island from becoming a Japanese possession, several prominent Formosan officials petitioned the Emperor to abrogate the Treaty. The Peking Government, however, advised the Formosans that it was committed to the Treaty and that Formosa could expect no help from the mainland.[2] The Formosan reaction to Peking's reply was the creation of the Formosan Democratic Republic. The new Republic was proclaimed on May 24, 1895.[3] The announcement was widely published in the hope that the World Powers would extend immediate recognition. Not wishing complete separation from China, the new government declared Formosa an independent state under the suzerainty of China.[4]

Neither the Japanese Government nor the World Powers heeded the Formosan plea for recognition. The Japanese dismissed the declarations of the new government as illegal and prepared to take the island by force. Japanese troops were landed at Aotikiong on May 30, 1895 and were immediately engaged in combat by the Formosans. Resistance to the occupation continued until the capture of Anping by the Japanese forces on October 21, 1895. The fall of Anping marked the end of the self-proclaimed Republic of Formosa.[5]

Formosa as a Province of China

Formosa was incorporated as a prefecture of the Province of Fukien in 1684 and remained in this status until 1885 when it received full provincial status. After 50 years of Japanese rule, the island was placed under the administration of the Republic of China. Shortly thereafter, on October, 1945, it was again incorporated as a province of China.

Some Formosans have objected to this apparent annexation of the island by China on the grounds that the Nationalist Government has no legal title to the territory.[6] Pursuing this argument, the spokesmen

[1] Liao, *op. cit.*, p. 11.
[2] Davidson, *op. cit.*, p. 277.
[3] Hosea B. Morse, " A Short Lived Republic," *New China Review*, Vol. 1, p. 27.
[4] Yosaburo Takekoshi, *Japanese Rule in Formosa*, (tr. by George Braithwaite), p. 83-84.
[5] Morse, *op. cit.*, p. 37.
[6] Liao, *op. cit.*, p. 1-3.

for Formosan independence have petitioned the United Nations to intervene in their behalf.[1] The Republic of China, however, has refused to discuss the issue on the grounds that the problem is an internal matter. As such, intervention by third parties would be a direct violation of Section 7, Article 2, of the United Nations Charter which states in part:

Nothing contained in the present Charter shall authorize the United Nations to intervene in matters which are essentially within the domestic jurisdiction of any state.[2]

From 1683 to 1895, Formosa was considered an integral part of China. Since 1945 it has been under the administration and *de facto* control of the Republic of China. The fact that the island was poorly administered during this time does not in any manner alter its status in law. It appears that the Formosan claim to independence, based on the arguments of misrule and long separation from China, is not legally valid.

Another cause for friction between the Formosans and the mainland Chinese is the charge by the Formosans of the utter lack of true democracy on the island. It is their complaint that:

The Formosans dominate all legislative bodies at the provincial level and below, and while the provincial governments run the day to day administration, they have no power to make any important policy decisions. These are made by the Central Government which is built on the hypothesis that it still controls the whole of China.[3]

The existence of two governmental mechanisms on the island—the provincial government of Formosa and the Central Government of China—should not in itself be a cause for dissension. Actually the political system that was established on the island was not different from that which had been operating on the mainland. The functions of the two governments are separate and have been established by law. In discussion of the constitutional position of the provincial government, Professor William Tung declared:

The provincial government of Taiwan is based upon the provisions of the 1946 Constitution and the *Revised Organic Law of the Provincial Government* of March 23, 1931, and is under the direct control of the National Government.[4]

At the present time, there are relatively few Formosans in high

[1] Chen I-te, "Formosa's Independence," *New York Times*, December 24, 1964, p. 26, Col. 4.

[2] United Nations, *Charter of the United Nations*, 1950, p. 5.

[3] Li Thian-hok, *op. cit.*, p. 439.

[4] William L. Tung, *The Political Institutions of Modern China*, p. 228.

position in the National Government. Popular election has not yet been applied to the officials of the provincial government. However, Professor Tung points out that the provincial and other officials of the local assemblies, as well as magistrates and mayors are elected by the local populace. In effect, "as far as local politics are concerned," it is safe to say that the Formosans are fairly represented.[1]

The structure of the National Government is essentially the same as that proposed by Dr. Sun Yat-sen.[2] Dr. Sun taught that the power to govern belonged to the people. However, the Chinese people throughout their history have been accustomed to autocratic rule and many have not yet grasped the full meaning of constitutionalism. Therefore, prior to the promulgation of the constitution, the power to govern was not vested in the people, but in the Central Executive Committee of the Kuomintang.[3]

A review of present constitutional practices of the National Government indicates that government leaders have occasionally resorted to some loose interpretations of the constitution in order to remain in power. In this connection, it might be recalled that President Chiang was re-elected in 1954 by the original National Assembly rather than by the new Assembly as prescribed by the constitution. In the 1960 elections President Chiang was elected to a third term by amending the pertinent provisions of the constitution which originally limited the President to two terms.

In the opinion of some observers, particularly the Formosan Nationalists, this type of legal maneuvering by the Kuomintang leaders renders the constitutionality of the National Government questionable. However, the legality of the National Government's actions can be justified by the existence of a national emergency since 1948.[4] In this connection, the "Temporary Provisions (to the constitution) Effective During the Period of Communist Rebellion," adopted by the National Assembly on April 18, 1948 and amended by the National Assembly on March 11, 1960 stipulate that:

> During the period of Communist Rebellion, the President and the Vice President may be re-elected without being subject to the two term restriction prescribed in Article 47 of the Constitution... The termination of the Period of Communist Rebellion shall be declared by the President.[5]

[1] *Ibid.*, p. 231.
[2] Pan Wei-tung, *The Chinese Constitution*, p. 66.
[3] For a full discussion of the Chinese National Government, see William L. Tung, *op. cit.*, p. 119-123, 218-227.
[4] *Ibid.*, p. 224-225.
[5] *The Constitution of the Republic of China, op. cit.*, p. 26.

It should be observed that constitutionalism as practiced in China differs in some respects from Western practice. However, the measures taken by the Kuomintang leaders in their efforts to maintain a united front in the continuing fight against Peiping appear to be justified. Under these circumstances, the constitutionality of the present National Government cannot be questioned, at least, not until the "Period of Communist Rebellion" is ended.

The Right of the Nationalist Government to establish its Seat on Formosa

The Formosans contend that the Nationalist Government forfeited its right to represent China when it failed to defeat the Chinese Communists. Pursuing this line of argument they have questioned the right of Chiang Kai-shek to establish the seat of his government on the island.

The transfer of the seat of the Nationalist Government to Formosa appears to be valid since Formosa was under *de facto* control of the Republic of China at that time. However, the claim that the Nationalist Government forfeited its right to represent the Chinese people does not appear to be logical since a state of war continues to exist between the rival factions. By its presence on Formosa the Republic of China leaves open the possibility, however remote at this time, that its forces will someday return to the mainland.

The Right of Self-Determination

Since the Formosans consider the present status of the island as undetermined, they have insisted on complete independence through a plebiscite in accordance with the principle and practice of self-determination.[1] To substantiate their claims, the Formosans cite the provisions of Article I of the United Nations Charter which states as one of its purposes:

> To develop friendly relations among nations based on respect for the principle of equal rights and self-determination of peoples.[2]

The Formosans claim that the right of self-determination was violated because the Cairo Declaration handed Formosa to China without consulting the Formosan people.[3] The Formosan argument appears questionable since the Cairo Declaration did not transfer title of the island from Japan to China.

[1] Liao, *op. cit.*, p. 55.
[2] *United Nations Charter, op. cit.*, p. 3.
[3] Li Thian-hok, *op. cit.*, p. 440.

The right of self-determination has been the subject of debate from time to time both in the General Assembly and the Security Council of the United Nations. As a rule, member states have supported the existence of such a right in law.

However, not all states agree with the doctrine of the right of self-determination. In fact, the present practice of some states dictates against the recognition of this alleged right. In his treatment on the subject Professor Starke has declared:

It may be seriously questioned what the expression of self-determination means or includes, and what tests are to be applied to determine what communities of human beings constitute "peoples" for the purpose of enjoying the alleged right... The process by which peoples or entities acquire statehood is preponderantly one governed by political considerations rather than by the application of legal principles.[1]

The correctness of Professor Starke's observations can be readily seen in the manner in which most nations have gained their independence since 1945. An important factor in the move for self-determination after World War II has been the tremendous surge of nationalism within these former colonial possessions. Such nations as Great Britain, France, and Portugal did not give up their colonial territories because of a belief in the right of self-determination. Basically, the prime considerations for colonial independence have been world opinions opposed to colonization and the fact that these once great powers are no longer strong enough to retain such territories.

Validity of Formosan Claims

The arguments presented by the Formosans in support of independence appear to be questionable in most instances.

Ethnically, the Formosans are of Chinese stock. Except for the 50 years of Japanese rule, the Formosans have been considered subjects of China and, consequently, owe obedience to its laws.

The Formosan claim that the Treaty of Shimonoseki was not legal because the island was ceded to Japan without the consent of the people appears to be questionable. In discussing forced cessions, Christian Wolf declared:

If by the treaty of peace either the entire sovereignty or a part of it is to be alienated... the king can make the alienation without the consent of the people.[2]

Although the consent of the people is desired and sometimes neces-

[1] Joseph G. Starke, *An Introduction to International Law.*, p. 105-106.
[2] Christian Wolf, *The Classics of International Law*, (tr. by Joseph H. Drake), Vol. 2, p. 510-511.

sary in the cession of territory,[1] the rule is generally dispensed with in treaties entered into as a result of the termination of war.[2] It follows, therefore, that under certain conditions the sovereign has the right to cede territory without the consent of his people.

Another argument advanced by the Formosans is that independence from China is possible on the basis of the proclamation of the Republic of Formosa in 1895. This argument does not appear valid since the Republic was proclaimed after the treaty of cession and without the approval of the Chinese Government. Further, as a result of the Treaty of Shimonoseki the Formosans became Japanese citizens and therefore subject to the laws of Japan.[3] Under these circumstances the Republic of Formosa, not being recognized as an international person, could exercise no rights in international law.[4]

There is little doubt that some of the complaints lodged against the Republic of China by the Formosans are justified and in need of remedy. However, these claims are of a moral nature and have no basis in legal precedent. The Formosans, as subjects of China, cannot take upon themselves an international character and seek independence through the intervention of the United Nations. The grievances of the Formosans are an internal Chinese matter, and the proper authorities for the redress of these grievances must be the Judicial Yuan and the Control Yuan of the Republic of China.

The Formosans' contention that the status of the island is yet to be determined remains a subject of controversy among the Allied Powers. The following chapter presents the opinions of those Powers most closely concerned in the controversy.

[1] L. Oppenheim, *International Law, A Treatise,* (ed. by H. Lauterpacht), Vol. 1, p. 551-552.

[2] Charles G. Fenwick, *International Law,* p. 262-263.

[3] Georg Schwarzenberger, *op. cit.*, p. 81.

[4] L. Oppenheim, *op. cit.*, p. 117-121.

V. INTERNATIONAL OPINIONS ON THE STATUS OF FORMOSA

The Peiping regime's claim to sovereignty over Formosa has resulted in a difference of opinion among the Allied Powers and among member states of the United Nations. Although some states, such as Great Britain[1] and India, have extended recognition to the Chinese Communist regime, they do not agree with its contention that Formosa is Chinese territory. The United States, although it has withheld recognition from Peiping, agrees with Great Britain and India that the Status of Formosa has not yet been determined.[2]

Conversely, the Republic of China which had occupied Formosa since 1945 does not agree with its allies and contends that Formosa is an integral part of China.[3] The controversy continues to this day and there does not appear to be a peaceful solution of the problem in the foreseeable future.

Furthermore, some member states of the United Nations in an effort to solve the problem have from time to time recommended the acceptance of the "Two China" theory, wherein both governments would be represented in the United Nations. However, the acceptance of the two China concept would not in itself solve the basic question of the legal status of the island.

The original intent of this work was to examine the legal opinions of the various States in an effort to present an objective survey of the problem. However, after extensive research was conducted on the subject, it was found that few states have rendered legal opinions on the Formosa question. Furthermore, the question has never been submitted to the International Court of Justice for review nor has that body rendered a legal opinion on the subject. In the light of these facts, an attempt is here made to present the attitudes of various states on the status of Formosa.

[1] D. H. N. Johnson, "Public International Law," *The British Year Book of International Law,* Vol. 39, 1952, p. 467.

[2] Edwin C. Hoyt, "The U.S. Reaction to the Korean Attack," *American Journal of International Law,* January 1961, Vol. 55, p.63.

[3] Chiang Kai-shek, "President Chiang Reviews World Situation," *Chinese News Service,* February 8, 1955, p. 3.

The British Position

On January 5, 1950, Great Britain recognized the Central People's Government of China as the *de jure* government of the Republic of China. By this act, Great Britain automatically ceased to recognize the Nationalist Government as the *de jure* government of the Republic of China. In stating Britain's policy in recognizing Communist China, the Undersecretary of State for Foreign Affairs, Mr. J. B. Godber, M.P., declared:

Generally speaking, it is the view of the Government that when, outside the existence of a state of war, a foreign Government are in obvious control of the territory which they claim to govern, they should be recognized as the Govern ment of the Country.[1]

It is evident from this statement that the British position is based on the assumption that Formosa is not Chinese territory. Pursuing this line of argument, the British contend that the Chinese Communists are in control of all Chinese territory. In support of his government's position, Sir Patrick Dean, the British Representative to the United Nations, declared:

that in view of Her Majesty's Government in the United Kingdom, sovereignty over the island of Formosa is undetermined.[2]

The British contend that the Cairo Declaration was a statement of purpose concurred in by Great Britain, China, and the United States at a time when the Nationalist Government was the sole claimant to the territory in question. Since the emergence of the Peiping regime, however, the question of Formosa has become international in scope and "cannot be solved merely by reference to the Cairo and Potsdam Declarations."[3]

Great Britain is also of the opinion that Formosa was legally ceded to Japan in accordance with the terms of the Treaty of Shimonoseki in 1895. Therefore, the allied statement in the Cairo Declaration that the territories stolen from China by Japan "shall be restored to China" could not include Formosa. Further, it was the Allied intention to retrocede Formosa to China after the war through the mechanics of a peace treaty between the Allied Powers and Japan. The fact that the

[1] J. B. Godber, M.P., "Chinese Representation in the United Nations," House of Commons London, *British Information Services*, 1960, p. 2.

[2] Sir Patrick Dean, "Chinese Representation," *United Nations*, General Assembly, Plenary Meeting, October 30, 1962, p. 1.

[3] E. Lauterpacht, "The Contemporary Practice of the United Kingdom In the Field of International Law," *The International and Comparative Law Quarterly*, Vol. 8, Part 1, January 1959, p. 186.

Republic of China accepted the Japanese surrender on Formosa, and that its representatives assumed administration of the island at the direction of the Supreme Allied Commander, did not in any way transfer title of the territory to China.[1]

It is the British contention that the retrocession of Formosa to the Republic of China has never taken place. Of significance to the British point of view is the fact that neither the Republic of China nor the Central People's Government of China were signatories to the San Francisco Peace Treaty of April 28, 1952.[2] In accordance with the terms of the Treaty, Japan formally renounced all right, title, and claim to Formosa. However, it is the British position that the renunciation did not in itself transfer sovereignty to either of the claimant Governments.[3]

The British also hold the opinion that the sovereignty of Formosa remained with Japan until the ratification of the San Francisco Treaty. The terms of the Treaty did not specify which of the claimant governments should receive title to the territory, nor was the island retroceded to either government. The renunciation constituted a dereliction of the territory by Japan and its status became subject to further arrangement among the Allied Powers.[4]

However, *de facto* dereliction of Formosa is said to have become effective on September 1, 1945 when Japan signed the Instrument of Surrender. The Republic of China was a signatory to this document and at that time the only claimant to the territory. In discussing the legal aspects of the Instrument of Surrender, Professor O'Connell stated:

> Japan accepted the provisions of the Potsdam Declaration and undertook to carry them out. The legal effect of this acceptance is by no means clear. It has been interpreted as a surrender of Japanese sovereignty over the areas specified in the Cairo Declaration, and with respect to Korea at least, subsequent decisions appear to have been based on that interpretation.[5]

In this instance, British policy in connection with the legal effect of the Instrument of Surrender appears to be inconsistent. In the case of Korea, the British Government did not raise any legal objections when

[1] E. Lauterpacht, "The Contemporary Practice of the United Kingdom in the Field of International Law," *The International and Comparative Law Quarterly*, Vol. 5, Part 5, July 1956, p. 413.

[2] Richard Harvey, "The Legal Status of Formosa," *World Affairs Quarterly*, Vol. 30, 1959-1960, p. 141.

[3] *Ibid.*, p. 414.

[4] J. P. Jain, "The Legal Status of Formosa," *American Journal of International Law*, Vol. 57, No. 1, January 1963, p. 28.

[5] D. P. O'Connell, "Legal Aspects of the Peace Treaty With Japan," *The British Year Book of International Law*, (ed. by E. Lauterpacht), Vol. 39, 1952, 0. 425.

that government was established in November 1947. However, in regard to Formosa, the British maintained the position that Japanese sovereignty was to terminate with the treaty of peace.[1] In examining the British attitude in this matter, it is difficult to understand how sovereignty of Korea passed from Japan to the Republic of Korea without the benefit of a peace treaty.

In support of its position on the status of Formosa, the British Government has contended that the parties to the San Francisco Peace Treaty are, in effect, exercising a condominium over Formosa. Therefore, the Republic of China is merely exercising a delegated authority on Formosa on behalf of the parties to the Peace Treaty, some of which continue to recognize that government as the legal government of China. In commenting on the British position relative to condominium, Professor Schwarzenberger declared:

> By Article 2(b) of the Treaty of Peace of San Francisco of 1951, Japan renounced "all right, title and claim to Formosa." This meant that, in relation to Japan, Formosa ceased to be Japanese territory and the other parties to the peace treaty had become the co-sovereigns of Formosa.[2]

The concept of condominium appears questionable since the signatories to the treaty did not choose to exercise this alleged right at the time of Japan's formal renunciation of the territory. Moreover, any attempt by the Allied Powers to exercise control over Formosa would, in the opinion of the Republic of China, constitute an act of intervention in its internal affairs.

Professor Schwarzenberger's theory of condominium has been considered as not legally valid and has been forcefully refuted by Professor Chao yin-ming in his article on "The Sovereignty of Taiwan From the Viewpoint of International Law".[3]

The Russian Position

The viewpoint of the Soviet Union is of special interest to this study since Communist China emerged as a power in the Far East as a result of Russian efforts. However, an examination of the official records of the United Nations, various journals of international law, and Russian newspapers as translated by the Tolstoy Foundation has failed to dis-

[1] D. P. O'Connell, *loc. cit.*

[2] Georg Schwarzenberger, "Letter to the Editor," *The Times*, London, February 2, 1955, Col. 5, p. 10.

[3] Chao yin-ming, "The Sovereignty of Taiwan From the Viewpoint of International Law," *Political Review*, Vol. 13, (Reprinted in the *Central Daily News*), March 4, 1965, p. 7.

close a definite Soviet position on the legal status of Formosa. Correspondence with the Soviet Mission to the United Nations and with the Soviet Embassy in Washington has proved fruitless since the Russian representatives have remained silent on the subject. Therefore, the only information available for examination and analysis consists of the statements of Soviet representatives to the United Nations that were made in connection with the "China Representation" question and were documented in the official records of that organization. The statements made by the various Soviet representatives are revealing and, in some instances, indicate the Soviet position on Formosa.

One of the first questions to be brought to the attention of the United Nations in connection with the emergence of Red China was Nationalist China's charge of Russian intervention in Chinese affairs. This question is the subject of further discussion in Chapter VI. However, during the initial discussion on Soviet intervention, the Soviet representative, Mr. Tajibaev, disclaimed the Nationalist charges on the grounds that the Kuomintang (the Nationalists) does not represent the Chinese people. In stating his Government's policy on China, Mr. Tajibaev declared:

> The Central People's Government of the People's Republic of China, is the only lawful government of China, which rules *de jure* and *de facto*.[1]

As had been expected during the early stages of the debates on China, the Soviet Union took the initiative in the Communist attempt to unseat the Republic of China in the United Nations.

The first indication of the Soviet Union's attitude on the status of Formosa came during the sixth session of the Federal Assembly when the China Representation question was again under discussion. At that time Mr. Jacob Malik, the Soviet representative, denied that Russia posed a threat to the political independence of China. According to Mr. Malik, the real threat to peace in the Far East was not manifested by Russia, but by the aggressive acts of the United States. Furthermore, in linking Formosa to mainland China he said:

> the United States... has committed innumerable acts of aggression against China, and has seized with its armed forces the Chinese island of Taiwan, which forms an inalienable part of China.[2]

Continuing his argument, Mr. Malik asserted that the Peiping regime enjoyed the unanimous support of all its people. In addition, it exer-

[1] A. Tajibaev, United Nations, General Assembly, *Official Records*, Fifth Session, September 26, 1950, p. 106-107.

[2] Jacob Malik, United Nations, General Assembly, *Official Records*, Sixth Session, November 13, 1951, p. 82.

cised full control over all Chinese territory with the exception of Formosa, which had been seized by United States forces. The Soviet Representative went on to say that the Peiping regime was a sovereign government and was free to control its own destiny. Any interference, therefore, with its right to exercise this prerogative was contrary to the principles of international law.

In clarifying its position on the China question, the Soviet Union contended that the conflict between the Chinese Communists and the Nationalist Government was an internal matter and, as such, was not subject to interference by third states. Therefore, as a sovereign nation, the Peiping government had the legal right to settle the Formosan question by any means which they chose. In speaking before the General Assembly on this subject, Andrei Vyshinsky said:

> to restrict the free exercise of this right by measures such as the decision which the General Committee is now trying to impose on us is... contrary to the Charter of the United Nations Organization which specifically condemns all intervention in matters coming within the domestic jurisdiction of other states.[1]

It was the Soviet opinion at that time that the United Nations should restore to the Peiping regime its legitimate rights, thus removing an injustice to that government and eliminating a violation of the charter. By so doing, the Communist regime could then take the necessary measures to restore Formosa to the Chinese people. However, the Russians contended that the restoration of Formosa to China could not be completed until the Republic of China was eliminated from the United Nations.[2]

In an obvious attempt to strengthen Communist China's claim to Formosa, the Soviet Union then extolled the peaceful intentions of the Chinese Communists. In speaking before the General Assembly, Mr. Sobolev, the Soviet Representative, assured that body that:

> the Peiping Government was ready to contribute to the settlement of controversial international issues including the question of liberating the Chinese island of Taiwan by peaceful means, that is, by negotiation.[3]

Accepting Mr. Sobolev's statement at face value, it would appear that the Soviet Union had changed its view and no longer considered the Formosan question an internal Chinese matter. However, the Soviet

[1] Andrei Vyshinsky, United Nations, General Assembly, *Official Records*, Sixth Session, November 13, 1951, p. 100.

[2] Vyacheslav Molotov, United Nations, General Assembly, *Official Records*, Tenth Session, September 20, 1955, p. 2-3.

[3] N. Sobolev, United Nations, General Assembly, *Official Records*, Eleventh Session, February 21, 1957, p. 1187.

Union again reversed its position after several years when it found that the majority of states did not agree with its views. In addressing the General Assembly during the Sixteenth Session, Valerin Zorin refuted any right of intervention in the internal affairs of China. In stating the views of this Government Mr. Zorin said:

The United Nations has nothing whatever to do with internal developments in China... It is not for the United Nations to discuss the internal problems which arise in a particular country nor to express views about them.[1]

Although the Russians tend to contradict themselves from time to time, it is evident that their position relative to the legal status of Formosa has been consistent. Basically, it is their contention that the Peiping regime is the rightful government of China and, consequently, has the legal right to all of China's territory, including Formosa. Furthermore, it is the opinion of the Soviet Union that Formosa is an inalienable part of Chinese territory. Finally, the Russians contend that the Formosan question is an internal Chinese problem and is not subject to the interference of third states.

The American Position

The Cairo Declaration marked the beginning of American policy concerning Formosa. Prior to the defeat of the Nationalist Government on the mainland, there appeared little doubt that the island would eventually be returned to Chinese sovereignty. However, with the emergence of Communist China, the United States reversed its original position on the status of the island and has since followed an inconsistent course.

An example of the inconsistency in American policy toward Formosa since 1949 can be seen in its refusal to recognize the Peiping regime and at the same time fail to support fully the Nationalist Government.[2]

After the Communist victory on the mainland, the United States was undecided as to the future of Formosa and its policy toward the Nationalist Government. After much deliberation, the United States announced that the conflict was an internal affair and that it would follow a policy of nonintervention. On January 5, 1950, in a public declaration in defense of the recently stated American policy on Chinese affairs, President Truman said:

[1] Valerin Zorin, United Nations, General Assembly, *Official Records*, Sixteenth Session, December 1, 1961, p. 873.

[2] N. I. Stone, "Policy on Red China," New York *Times*, February 3, 1955, Col. 6, p. 22.

In keeping with these declarations (Cairo and Potsdam), Formosa was surrendered to Generalissimo Chiang Kai-shek, and for the past four years, the United States and the other Allied Powers have accepted the exercise of Chinese authority over the island.[1]

Shortly after the President's statement on China, Secretary of State Dean Acheson clarified the Government's position on the status of Formosa. In an effort to dispel any doubts on Chinese title to the island the Secretary said:

When Formosa was made a province of China nobody raised any lawyers' doubts about that. That was regarded in accordance with the commitments.[2]

Some months later, United States policy toward Formosa underwent an abrupt reversal when, in June 1950, the North Korean Communists crossed the 38th parallel and invaded South Korea. In order to protect the American military perimeter, President Truman ordered the United States Seventh Fleet into the Formosa Straits. Thus, in a complete reversal of his statement of the previous January and in the name of the United Nations, the President was intervening in the internal affairs of China. The American position was amplified in the President's message to Congress of July 19, 1950, when he stated that the military neutralization of Formosa was without prejudice to political questions affecting that island. "Our desire," the message said, "is that all questions affecting Formosa be settled by peaceful means as envisaged in the charter of the United Nations.[3]

The Chinese Communists took immediate issue with the President's decision to protect Formosa. The United States was charged with aggression against China because of its intervention in Chinese domestic affairs. In speaking before the Security Council, Ernest Gross, the American Representative, defended the United States' action against Communist China's charges. In a reversal of American policy, he argued that:

The actual status of the island is that it is territory taken from Japan by the victory of the Allied Forces in the Pacific. Like other such territories, its legal status cannot be fixed until there is international action to determine its future. The Chinese Government was asked by the Allies to take the surrender of the Japanese forces on the island. That is the reason the Chinese are there now.[4]

[1] Edwin C. Hoyt, "The United States Reaction to the Korean Attack," *American Journal of International Law*, January 1961, Vol. 55, p. 61.

[2] Dean Acheson, "U.S. Policy Toward Formosa," *Department of State Bulletin*, Vol. 22, p. 80.

[3] Benjamin H. Brown, "Chinese Representation: A Case Study in United Nations Political Affairs," *United Nations*, September 1955, p. 7.

[4] Ernest Gross, United Nations, Security Council, *Official Records*, 490th Meeting, August 25, 1950, p. 7.

Both the National Government and the Chinese Communists rejected the American contention that Formosa was not Chinese territory. In this connection, Professor William L. Tung, a recognized authority of both international law and of Far Eastern affairs, declared: "While the Nationalists and Communists have been irrevocably antagonistic to each other, they do agree that Taiwan is an integral part of China and that there should never be two Chinas." After analyzing the legal status of the Formosans and of the Mainlanders, he further concluded that "any scheme of creating a Taiwanese State is both unconstitutional and impractical."[1] The National Government considers the island as an integral part of Chinese territory and a bastion from which it will someday return to the mainland. On the other hand, the Chinese Communists consider the island Chinese territory in the possession of its enemies which must be liberated.

Toward the end of 1955, the Chinese Communists began a bombardment of the coastal islands of Quemoy and Matsu. It appeared likely that the Peiping regime would make good its earlier threat to take Formosa by force. President Eisenhower, in an effort to effect a cease-fire and to protect the island from falling into Communist hands, requested that the Congress approve a resolution authorizing the use of military force in the Formosa Straits.

The President's request was considered in the Congress, and after some debate, House Joint Resolution 159 was passed. The resolution gave the President extremely broad latitude of decision with respect to taking action to defend Formosa and the offshore islands.[2]

House Joint Resolution 159 and the New Zealand proposal to the Security Council, which requested a consideration by the United Nations of the threat to peace in the Formosa area, were met by strong reaction from the Communist Chinese. In connection with the proposal by New Zealand, the Peiping regime refused an invitation by the Secretary General to participate in United Nations discussions on the matter. In commenting on the proposal, Chou En-lai declared:

> The New Zealand resolution was not within the competence of the United Nations because the liberation of Formosa and other coastal islands was a matter of "sovereign rights" and an internal affair.[3]

The opinions of the Peiping regime were shared by the Russian Government, which considered President Eisenhower's resolution to be

[1] Tung, *op. cit.*, p. 235; see also Harvey, *op. cit.*, p. 134.
[2] Maurer, *op. cit.*, p. 1006-1007.
[3] *Ibid.*

an instrument of American intervention in Chinese affairs. Some observers such as Derek Bodde have questioned the legality of the American action in the Formosa Straits. In commenting on the subject Mr. Bodde stated:

The conflict between the two was a civil war today. By what conceivable moral right then, do we... presume to tell this government Communist though it may be, what it may or may not do about areas which we ourselves (at the 1943 Cairo Conference) have declared to be part of China?[1]

Some observers do not consider the Peiping regime as the legal government of China.[2] They consider the Chinese Communists as usurpers who have seized control of the government by illegal means and without the consent of the Chinese people. These observers cite the inconsistency in the American position toward the Nationalist Government and the status of Formosa. Their main objection to President Eisenhower's resolution is the fact that it enables the United States to interfere in the internal affairs of China. That is, by supporting a cease-fire agreement in the Formosa area, the United States is acting against the expressed wishes of the Nationalist Government to abide by such an agreement, "we are giving up and are forcing that Government to give up all efforts to overthrow the Communist usurper."[3]

The United States has long recognized the fact that the Chinese Communists could not have attained control over the mainland without outside aid. It is also aware that this aid came from Russia in violation of its treaty with the Nationalist Government. Despite this knowledge, the United States has recognized that the Peiping regime is in *de facto* control of the mainland. However, it has refused to extend diplomatic recognition to that government on moral rather than legal grounds.

Further, the United States considers the question of recognition and the legal status of Formosa as separate issues. In refuting the Chinese Communist claims to the island, Secretary of State Dulles declared:

The Chinese Communist regime has never during its nine years of existence exercised any authority over Taiwan, the Penghu, or the Quemoy or Matsu islands.[4]

According to Mr. Dulles, the Chinese Communists were trying to extend their authority over these islands by the use of naked force.

[1] Derek Bodde, "Interference in Civil War seen," New York *Times*, February 3, 1955, Col. 6, p. 22.

[2] Joseph Grew, "Support of Taiwan Urged," New York *Times*, October 31, 1958, Sec. 4, Col. 5, p. 8.

[3] Stone, *op. cit.*, Col. 6, p. 22.

[4] John Foster Dulles, "Problems of Peace and Progress," *Department of State Bulletin*, Vol. 39, 1958, p. 525.

In defense of its position on the status of Formosa, the United States does not agree that the San Francisco Peace Treaty, or any other treaty transferred title of the island from Japan to the Republic of China. According to the United States, there has been no definite cession of Formosa to China. "The situation is, then, one where the Allied Powers still have to come to some agreement or treaty with respect to the status of Formosa."[1]

It follows that the United States does not consider Formosa as Chinese territory. Therefore, it is the opinion of the United States that any attempt by the Chinese Communists to seize Formosa would be a violation of international law and of the Charter of the United Nations. Therefore, as an Allied Power, the United States considers itself to be within its legal right in taking action to defend the island.

The Japanese Position

The views of the Japanese Government on the status of Formosa are considered important to this study since the island was under Japanese sovereignty for fifty years before relinquishing *de facto* control of the territory in 1945.

In reply to several questions related to the status of Formosa, Ambassador Katsuo Okazaki, Permanent Representative to the Permanent Mission of Japan to the United Nations explained that his Government was not in the position to render an opinion on the subject since "it has never been discussed at the United Nations."[2]

However, at the Sixteenth Session of the General Assembly, on December 6, 1961, Ambassador Okazaki, in discussing the China Representation question, made a direct reference to the status of Formosa when he declared:

> By the Peace Treaty which was signed at San Francisco between Japan and the Allied Powers on September 8, 1951, Japan renounced all right, title, and claim to Taiwan and the neighboring Pescadores Islands. At the present time, Taiwan, ... holds, of course, the seat of the Government of the Republic of China and the Central People's Republic of China has never extended its actual control over the area.[3]

It is evident that Ambassador Okazaki's statement was made in reply to Red China's claim to Formosa. There appears to be little

[1] Maurer, *op. cit.*, p. 1009.

[2] Y. Nakae, First Secretary, Permanent Mission of Japan to the United Nations, Letter dated February 19, 1964, p. 1.

[3] Katsuo Okazaki, United Nations, General Assembly, *Official Records*, Sixteenth Session, 1072 Plenary Meeting, December 6, 1961, p. 943-946.

question that the Japanese Government has rejected the Peiping regime's argument that it has legal right to sovereignty over Formosa.

The Indian Position

The viewpoint of the Indian Government is of special interest to this study for several reasons. In the first instance, India, in an effort to protect itself from invasion, has pursued a policy of appeasement toward Communist China. The second reason is that India, in declaring a policy of neutralism, had hoped to be the most influential nation in Asia. Finally, in an effort to maintain the peace, India quickly extended recognition to the Peiping regime.

In pursuing its policy of appeasing Communist China, India has long supported its admission into the United Nations. India's former Representative to the United Nations V. K. Krishna Menon often acted as the spokesman for Communist China.

The Indian Government's views on the legal status of Formosa suffered a reversal in the five and a half years from September 1950 to February 1955. Shortly after the defeat of the Nationalist Government, India was of the opinion that the problem of Formosa could be settled by properly interpreting the intentions of the Cairo Declaration. In discussing the subject in the General Assembly, the Indian Representative Sir Benegal Rau said:

> Formosa was considered as a "Former Japanese" territory regarding whose disposal there have been certain declarations in the past, but whose actual disposal still remains te bo made.[1]

With this statement, India rejected the claims of both Communist China and the Nationalist Government.

According to the views of the Indian Government, sovereignty did not pass from Japan to the Republic of China upon Japan's acceptance of the terms of surrender. Similarly, Formosa did not retrocede to China as a result of China's unilateral abrogation of all treaties between the two countries prior to 1941, as the Chinese Communists claimed.

India's previous position on the legal status of Formosa changed in February, 1955, when Communist China renewed its campaign to seize the island by force. The question of Formosa was discussed in the Indian Parliament. In support of Communist China, the President of India stated that Communist China's claims to Formosa were justified. On the same day, Premier Jawaharlal Nehru, in his statement to the

[1] Sir Benegal N. Rau, United Nations, General Assembly, *Official Records*, 286th Plenary Meeting, September 27, 1950, p. 134.

Parliament, agreed with the President's earlier statement when he declared:

Chinese claims are justified. According to our thinking because we cannot recognize two China's because Formosa has been part of the Chinese state for hundreds and hundreds of years... except for a little less than half a century when the Japanese occupied it, and also because it was clearly stated in the Cairo and Potsdam Declarations that Formosa should go to China.[1]

Premier Nehru's statement reveals for the first time India's interpretation of the Cairo and Potsdam Declarations. The disposal of Formosa in accordance with certain declarations, as stated by Sir Benegal Rau in the General Assembly on September 27, 1950, is now interpreted as a retrocession of the island to China. However, Premier Nehru neglected to point out that the China that signed the Cairo and Potsdam Declarations is the Republic of China, which occupies Formosa at the present time.

In clarifying the new Indian position on Formosa, Mr. V. K. Krishna Menon, former Ambassador to the United Nations, claimed that "Formosa and Manchuria were not placed under trusteeship, but were liberated and made part of China."[2] Furthermore, the Indian Government now took the position that the conflict between the Republic of China and the Peiping regime was an internal matter. In discussing the subject in the General Assembly, Mr. Menon said:

My Government... pleads not for any intervention by the United Nations, because I do not see how that is possible. For one thing, the United Nations has tied its hands for a year by refusing to discuss it... But over and above that, it is not an international problem.[3]

The change in the Indian Government's attitude appears to have been motivated by political expediency rather than by law. It should be observed that the Indian attitude underwent a further change after Communist China attacked India, after Nehru's death, and after the Communist Chinese set off an atomic explosion in October 1964. Since these three incidents, India has not sponsored Communist China's entry into the United Nations. It is significant that in all the attempts made to solve the Formosan question, no member state of the United Nations had proposed to refer the question to the International Court of Justice for a legal opinion.

[1] Jain, *op. cit.*, p. 41.

[2] V. K. Krishna Menon, United Nations, General Assembly, *Official Records*, Thirteenth Session, 774 Plenary Meeting, October 7, 1958, p. 369.

[3] *Ibid.*, p. 370.

The Irish Position

Shortly after the Communist Chinese set off a nuclear device in October 1964, the Irish position on the status of Formosa was clarified by that government's representative in the United Nations.

The Irish Government concerned by the Communist Chinese atomic explosion and its possible effect on world peace, has proposed that the People's Republic of China be admitted as a permanent member of the security council. The Communist regime at Peiping would, of course, replace the Nationalist Government in the Council. In turn, Formosa would take a seat in the General Assembly and retain membership in the United Nations. In effect, the Irish Government has proposed a "one-China and one-Taiwan" policy.

It should be observed that the Irish Government does not make any reference to the Nationalist Government of China or of the fact that that government now holds a permanent seat in the Security Council. Further, the Irish Government has implied that Formosa is currently under Chinese occupation and that its twelve million people seek to govern themselves.[1]

In discussing the subject in the General Assembly, Mr. Aiken, the Irish Representative, said:

> I do not know, of course, whether it would be possible to negotiate an agreed settlement of the problem which is called the representation of China. I suggest, however, that the Secretary-General and the four nuclear Powers in the Security Council should be asked to negotiate with Peking and Taiwan between now and the next session to find out whether agreement could be arrived at on the following basis: that Taiwan would take a seat in the Assembly and that Peking would assume the position of a permanent member of the Security Council, accepting to be bound by the Purposes and Principles of the Charter, by a nondissemination agreement and by an agreement that all other nuclear states would go to the assistance of a non-nuclear state attacked by a nuclear power.[2]

It is evident that the Irish Government has based its argument on the Conlon Report of November 1, 1959, and on the fact that Ireland now considers the Communist Government of Peiping as the world's fifth nuclear power. What has escaped the Irish Government at this time is the fact that the so-called "Two-China Theory" has been flatly rejected by both Taipei and Peiping on many occasions. Furthermore, the representatives of the Nationalist Government have repeatedly rejected the "Two-China Theory" in the General Assembly and in the

[1] Frank Aiken, United Nations, General Assembly, *Official Records*, Plenary Meeting of the 19th Session, (A/PV 1295), December 8, 1964, p. 13-15.

[2] *Ibid.*, p. 16.

Security Council on numerous occasions. In essence, it appears that the Irish proposal is based on a political solution to a legal problem.

The Two-China Theory

In an attempt to help solve the Formosan problem, some nations have proposed what has come to be known as the "Two-China Theory." The leading proponent of this theory in the United Nations has been Great Britain; however, other nations such as India, Ceylon, and Ireland have found in it a possible solution to a complex problem and have proposed various versions of the theory.

Basically, the two-China concept involves the recognition of the Communist government as the legal representative of the Chinese state and as being entitled to the Republic of China's seat in the Security Council. The Republic of China would be recognized as a new state and be known as the Republic of Formosa. Although the new state would be admitted to the United Nations, it would not have a seat in the Security Council.[1]

The acceptance of the two-China concept would create several problems for the United Nations and for the claimant entities. First, it is questionable at this time whether the Republic of China would consent to a surrender of its seat in the United Nations in favor of Peiping; nor is it likely to relinquish its right to represent the Chinese people. In addition, unless the United Nations Charter is amended, it is not quite clear how two China's could be accepted into the United Nations under its present provisions. From what has been said thus far, it is evident that the two-China concept provides neither a simple nor a quick solution to the Formosan problem. In view of these facts, the positions of various states have been examined to determine the validity of their proposals.

The British Government, in an effort to maintain the status quo in the Far East, has publicly supported the two-China concept. The British believe that the two-China concept can be made to work if the two rivals agree to accept the present status of their governments and not seek the territory of the other. In support of their arguments, the British hold that neither Cairo nor any other international agreement or treaty transferred title of the territory to either of the claimant entities.[2] Pursuing this argument, the British contend that the matter

[1] Arthur H. Dean, "International Law and Current Problems in the Far East," *Proceedings of the American Society of International Law*, April 1955, p. 87.

[2] *Cf. supra*, p. 3.

is one of international concern and is subject to discussion in the United Nations.

It is the opinion of the British Government, therefore, that the United Nations has the right to settle the question of Formosan sovereignty by placing the island under trusteeship and holding a plebiscite at a later date or by accepting the two-China concept.[1]

The British position has been challenged by Li Tze-chung in his letter to the editor of the New York Times. In refuting the British argument, Mr. Li contends that all Chinese consider Formosa as an integral part of China. As such, the problem of Formosa is a domestic one, and not subject to consideration by the United Nations. Mr. Li further contends that the suggested method of a plebiscite through the United Nations would violate Article 2, Paragraph 7 of the United Nations Charter which provides that "Nothing contained in the present charter shall authorize the United Nations to intervene in matters which are essentially within the domestic jurisdiction of any state.[2]

Acceptance of the British proposal by the Republic of China does not appear likely at the present time. Acceptance would magnify the international status of the Peiping regime and would eventually lead to its recognition.[3] The Republic of China has done its utmost to avoid this possibility.

In accepting the British proposal of the two-China concept Sir John Kotelawala, Prime Minister of Ceylon, speaking for the Colombo Powers, presented his plan for the settlement of the Formosa question. The Prime Minister's plans called for a five-year trusteeship of the island by either the United Nations or the Colombo Powers to replace the present administration. After five years, the Formosans would vote in a plebiscite to choose the form of their government.[4]

The proposition by the Allied Powers that Formosa could be placed under United Nations trusteeship is questionable in view of the fact that the Nationalist Government has been in *de facto* control of the island since 1945. At that time, the Nationalist administration of the island was considered proper and legal. The United Nations also failed to take action on the administration of Formosa after Japan renounced title to the territory as a result of the San Francisco Peace Treaty.

[1] Jain, *op. cit.*, p. 30.
[2] Li Tze-Chung, "Against Formosa Plebiscite," *New York Times*, December 10, 1964, Col. 6, p. 29; see also Tung, *op. cit.*, p. 234-35.
[3] Arthur H. Dean, "United States Foreign Policy and Formosa," *Foreign Affairs*, April 1955, Vol. 33, p. 370-372.
[4] Sir John Kotelawala, "Colomban Plan," *New York Times*, April 22, 1955, Col. 4, p. 2.

It is not clear how an action which was considered legal in 1945 and in 1952 could be considered illegal by the Allied Powers at the present time, particularly since the legal factors in the case remain the same. It should be observed that legal questions cannot and should not be resolved through the use of political expediencies.

The alternative proposal, which would delegate administrative control of the island to the Colombo Powers, does not appear to be legal. These Powers, consisting of Burma, Ceylon, India, Indonesia, and Pakistan, were not signatories to either the Cairo Declaration or the Potsdam Proclamation. Under these circumstances, they had no voice in the Allied Powers decision on the future status of Formosa. The fact that the Colombo Powers are now member states of the United Nations does not give them the legal right to assume administrative control over the territory of a sovereign power without the consent of that power.

Although the United States has not openly supported the two-China concept it has, from time to time, attempted to test public reaction by hinting at the possible recognition of Communist China. One such test occurred in January 1955, when President Eisenhower, referring to the explosive situation in the Formosa Straits, declared that he "envisaged the possibility of settling the problem of China by recognizing the existence of two China's."[1]

Public reaction to the President's statement was relatively mild and in some instances favorable. Arthur Dean, in reviewing the two-China concept in connection with the continuity of the legal order of states, openly wondered if Nationalist China, being recognized as a new state, would be the same Republic of China. In commenting Mr. Dean declared:

> Certainly, if as has been urged by some writers, the continuity of the legal order is the most important element in the identity of the state, the state represented by the Nationalist Government might well be regarded as identical with the old China.[2]

Mr. Dean's statement is significant and appears valid since the Republic of China, as represented by the Nationalist Government, has been recognized as the representative of the Chinese people since 1927. The fact that it occupies disputed territory should not detract from that Government's international character.

[1] Quincy Wright, "The Chinese Recognition Problem," *The American Journal of International Law*, Vol. 49, No. 2, April 1955, p. 320.

[2] Dean, *Proceedings of the American Society of International Law.*, *op. cit.*, p. 87.

Some writers, such as Bronson W. Chandler, are of the opinion that the Nationalist Government has lost the war and should no longer be recognized as the legal representative of the Chinese people. Furthermore, he does not approve of the two-China concept and proposes the creation of Formosa as an independent republic. Although Mr. Chandler is not clear as to which of the claimant entities should have the right to China's overseas assets and jurisdiction over Chinese citizens who have not renounced Chinese citizenship, he declares:

> This new Government could be called "Formosan" pure and simple, so that the unrealistic name of "Nationalist Chinese" could disappear from our current usage.[1]

In effect, what Mr. Chandler has advocated is that the Republic of China lose its identity and become un-Chinese by legislation.

A similar position has been taken by John Carter Vincent. Mr. Vincent has also opposed the two-China concept. However, the basis for his argument is that Formosa is not China, nor is it recognized as a part of China in the Japanese Peace Treaty. As an alternative to the two-China concept, Mr. Vincent proposes the recognition of the Peiping regime and the formation of the Republic of Taiwan, "whose independence would be recognized and underwritten by the United Nations and defended, if necessary, by the United States."[2]

Aside from the legal problems involved, Mr. Vincent's proposal is not realistic. The implication behind Mr. Vincent's proposal is that Communist China, after it has achieved recognition and replaced the Republic of China in the United Nations, will continue in its attempts to seize Formosa. It is evident that Mr. Vincent's proposal would not solve the Formosan question. The only actual change that would take place would be the withdrawal of recognition from the Republic of China and its expulsion from the United Nations. No state could guarantee that a Communist China with a veto power would agree to admit the Republic of China, which has had its name changed to the Republic of Taiwan, into the United Nations.

The Conlon Report

The most significant work published in connection with the Two-China concept is the Conlon report. This work has served as the basis for the American and Irish positions on the status of Formosa.

[1] Bronson W. Chandler, "New Status for Formosa," *New York Times*, February 1, 1955, Col. 8, p. 7.

[2] John Carter Vincent, "The Two-China Plan Opposed," *New York Times*, December 17, 1961, Col. 5, p. 8.

As cited earlier, the United States has never taken a definite position concerning the two-China concept.[1] However, statements made by the President of the United States and the Secretary of State indicate that under the proper circumstances, the United States would entertain the two-China concept. Giving substance to the American attitude on the two-China theory is the Conlon Associates Report based on American foreign policy in Asia. The study, sponsored by the Senate Committee on Foreign Relations on February 16, 1959, was completed in the summer of the same year and submitted to the Senate Committee on September 1. The report is most comprehensive and entails a study of the geographical areas of Asia. It includes the Associates' observations and recommendations in each area studied by its investigators. For the purposes of this study however, examination of the Conlon Report will be limited to the Associate's recommendations concerning its studies of Communist China and Formosa.

The Conlon Associates Report offered the United States three major alternatives in meeting Far Eastern problems that have arisen as a result of the China representation question. These policy alternatives are: (1) containment of Communist China through isolation, (2) normalization of relations with the Chinese Communists, and (3) exploration and negotiation with Communist China.[2]

The report strongly recommended the adoption by the United States of step three. Acceptance of the Conlon Associates recommendations would mean eventual American recognition of the Peiping regime. Moreover, Communist China would be classed as a major world Power and be accorded the same courtesies as the United States extends to the Soviet Union. Most significant, however, is the recommendation that the United States accept the two-China concept.

In its argument for American acceptance, the Conlon Report emphasized that the continued recognition of the Nationalist Government as the only legitimate government of China is not realistic. Furthermore, Communist China belongs in the United Nations. Its membership in the organization would do much to stabilize the situation in the Far East.[3]

In recommending the acceptance of the two-China concept, the report suggested that Communist China would be admitted to the

[1] *Cf. supra*, p. 25.

[2] United States Congress, Foreign Relations Committee, "United States Foreign Policy in Asia," *The Conlon Report*, Study No. 5, San Francisco, September 1949, p. 547, ff (Hereafter referred to as *Conlon Report*).

[3] *Ibid.*, p. 548 ff.

United Nations. In addition, the Republic of China would be recognized as the Republic of Formosa and would be seated in the General Assembly. The Charter of the United Nations would then be revised to include India and Japan as permanent members of the Security Council. Finally, the military forces of Formosa would be withdrawn from the offshore islands. The United States would continue to honor its existing obligations to Formosa and the Pescadores and would underwrite the defense of the Republic of Formosa.[1]

Basically, the Conlon report appears to be a reiteration of the views expressed by Great Britain, the Colomban Powers, and such writers as Bronson W. Chandler and John Carter Vincent. It is evident from the recommendations made in the report that the persons who wrote it are extremely idealistic and have not considered the Formosan question from a realistic point of view. It is also evident that the Conlon Associates have learned nothing from United States relations with Russia or from Communist China's actions since 1949.

Of greatest significance, however, is the complete disregard for the legal principles of international law contained in the Conlon Associates' recommendation about the recognition of the two-China concept. To seat the Chinese Communists in the Security Council in place of the Republic of China would be a grave injustice to the latter Government. However, to admit Peiping into the United Nations in the first place would be a violation of the basic principles of the Charter, specifically Article Four, which states:

> Membership in the United Nations is open to all other peace loving states which accept the obligations contained in the present Charter and, in the judgement of the organization are able and willing to carry out these obligations.[2]

The two-China concept does not appear to be legally valid since it has been the practice of states not to recognize two entities representing the same people. The legal status of Formosa involves considerably more than the right to sovereignty over the island. It is entwined with the right of the Nationalist Government to continue in existence and with the legitimacy of the Peiping regime. The rights and claims of these two governments are treated in subsequent chapters. The Conlon Report made no mention of these facts, nor did it recommend a study of the Formosan problem by the International Court of Justice or by any other international tribunal.

[1] *Ibid.*, p. 549.

[2] United Nations, *Charter of the United Nations*, United Nations Office of Public Information, p. 6.

The two-China concept, although it has been proposed by several nations as a solution to the Formosan problem, has not been acceptable to either the Republic of China or the Peiping regime. Both claimants have considered the problem an internal matter of China and resent any outside interference or discussion of the subject. In commenting on United Nations participation in the Formosan question, Premier Chou En-lai expressed the opinions of Communist China when he observed:

> All proposals to place Taiwan under United Nations trusteeship... or to create a so-called independent Taiwan state, are attempts to carve up China's territory, enslave the Chinese people on Taiwan and legalize United States occupation of Taiwan. None of these will be tolerated by the Chinese people.[1]

The Chinese Communists further expressed their views in an editorial in the Peoples Daily (Jenmin Jihpao), the official Chinese Communist organ, published on May 12, 1964. In that instance the Peiping Government accused the United States of trying to detach Taiwan from China when it stated:

> The "one China and one Taiwan" scheme is nothing but a variation of the "two-Chinas." They have the same aim of detaching the province of Taiwan from China, legalizing the permanent U.S. occupation of the island and turning it into a U.S. Colony... It is China's internal affair for the Chinese people to liberate their own Taiwan province; no one has the right to interfere in this.[2]

It is evident that the Peiping regime is of the belief that neither the United States nor the United Nations have the right to discuss the Formosan question nor to interfere in the internal affairs of China.

Although the Republic of China and the Peiping regime disagree on many matters, they agree on opposing the two-China concept. In a speech to high Government officials at Taipei on February 8, 1955, President Chiang Kai-shek reviewed the situation in the Formosa Strait. In discussing the two-China concept, he declared:

> We have also heard about the ridiculous view of "Two Chinas." This is simply absurd. I would like to ask those people holding such views whether, if unhappily Soviet Russia should invade their countries and install Quisling regimes on their soil, they would still be prepared to swallow the reality of having their countries cut into halves.[3]

Despite President Chiang's strong opposition to the two-China concept, there are those observers such as Chester Bowles who, in the

[1] Jain, *op. cit.*, p. 36.
[2] Republic of China, "Background On China," *Chinese News Service*, (Editorial by *The People's Daily*, Peiping Opposes, 'One China on Taiwan' plot, May 12, 1964), p. 1-4.
[3] Chiang Kai-shek, Documentary, "President Chiang Reviews World Situation," *China News Service*, February 5, 1955, p. 4.

interest of Asian security, would set an independent Formosa as an example to Asian Nations. In discussing the two-China concept, Mr. Bowles said:

An independent Sino-Formosan nation can offer the contrast of a modernized non-Communist Chinese society free from mass regimentation, with an increasing measure of political liberty and with expanding economic opportunities for all citizens.[1]

In direct rebuttal to those who support the two-China concept, Dr. Paul K. T. Sih declared:

The free China Government is physically in control of the territory of Formosa and its present source of political order. To alter this without first consulting the government and the people is high-handed imperialism not only in Chinese eyes but also to the entire Asian world. The United States can hardly favor such action. Free China is our ally not our satellite. So long as Free China opposes the creation of a Sino-Formosan state, no one else could impose such a plan on her.[2]

According to Dr. Sih, the creation of a Republic of Taiwan, without the expressed consent of the Republic of China, would be a violation of international law. It is the position of the Nationalist Government that it continues to exist on its own territory and that third states cannot interfere in its internal affairs.

The Soviet Union has also expressed its disapproval of the two-China concept. However, its reasons are not quite the same as those expressed by President Chiang and Dr. Sih. During discussions on the China representation question, Andrei Gromyko, the Soviet representative observed:

however much the apologists for United States aggression against China may try to underpin that aggression with some sort of "theoretical foundation" in the form of the spurious "Two-Chinas" formula they have invented, China always has been and still is China, while the island of Taiwan... is an inalienable part of Chinese territory.[3]

In a similar speech to the General Assembly, I. Shepilov, the Soviet Representative, also denounced the two-China concept as illegal. In commenting on the subject, Mr. Shepilov said:

In actual fact, there have never been and there are not now two-Chinas... there is but one China... Those who have the audacity to suggest the representation

[1] Chester Bowles, "The China Problem Reconsidered," *Foreign Affairs*, April 1960, Vol. 38, No. 3, p. 480-481.

[2] Dr. Paul K. T. Sih, "Two-Chinas: Fact and Myth," *National Catholic Welfare Council*, p. 5.

[3] Andrei Gromyko, United Nations, General Assembly, *Official Records*, Thirteenth Session, 753 Plenary Meeting, September 22, 1958, p. 62.

of two Chinas in the United Nations are in fact trying to induce the United Nations to fabricate a second China.[1]

It is evident that the Soviet Union, in expressing its objections to the two-China concept, has not resorted to legal principles to support its arguments. It has objected to the two-China concept on the ground that Formosa is Chinese territory of which Communist China is the rightful sovereign. If this line of argument is to be accepted, the two-China concept is reduced to an absurdity because there is only one China and that is the Peiping regime, supported by Russia.

In examining the attitudes of the various states in connection with the legal status of Formosa and the two-China concept, it is evident that the majority of states have based their arguments on self-interest and national security rather than on law. All the positions examined thus far on the legal status of Formosa appear to be questionable and are in need of judicial review and interpretation by the International Court of Justice. To present the problem to the Security Council or to the General Assembly for solution would be to no avail since the questions decided in those organs are based on political expediency rather than on law. Insofar as the two-China concept is concerned, there is no legal basis in international law for the creation of a second China.

One of the most effective refutations of the Conlon Report is contained in an unpublished paper by Lin Yutang and other Chinese scholars. In their paper the Chinese scholars question the objectivity of the Conlon Associates in connection with such issues as: (1) the elimination of the Republic of China, (2) the creation of a Republic of Taiwan, (3) the representation of Communist China in the United Nations in place of the Republic of China, and (4) a permanent seat in the Security Council for Communist China in place of the Republic of China.[2]

In commenting on the recommendations of the Conlon Report, the Chinese scholars were of the opinion that:

the findings of the report are full of self-contradictions and tendentious reasoning. Their arguments are reminiscent of the Communist dialectics which borders on sophistry.[3]

The Chinese scholars further contend that the "exploration and negotiation policy" recommended by the Conlon Associates reveals the

[1] Igor Shepilov, United Nations, General Assembly, *Official Records*, Eleventh Session, 578 Plenary Meeting, November 15, 1956, p. 47-49.

[2] Lin Yutang, An Analysis of the Conlon Report: *Its Fallacies and Contradictions as viewed by Asians*, 1960, p. 4.

[3] *Loc. cit.*, p. 4.

fact that their understanding of the situation in the Far East, particularly in Communist China and Formosa, is erroneous and their conclusions are injurious to the interest of the United States. In effect, it is a policy based on a lack of realism.[1]

In discussing the recommendation of the Conlon Report that a plebiscite be held on Formosa, the Chinese scholars contend that there is no racial and cultural difference between the Formosans and the mainland refugees. Whatever differences of opinion may exist between the two groups, they are no more than those that would arise between two provinces of the same country, nothing more. Furthermore, the suggestion of holding a plebiscite in order to determine Formosa's independence seems absurd. This is true particularly since no suggestion has been made to hold a plebiscite in Communist China.[2]

In discussing the "one China and one Taiwan" concept, the Chinese scholars contend that "the title of the 'Republic of China' is inaugurated through the bloody sacrifice of numerous martyrs under the leadership of Sun Yat-sen."[3] The Nationalist Government could never consent to substitute this title for that of the "Republic of Taiwan." The Chinese scholars also point out that today there are two German, two Viet-Nam and two Korean states.

To date, no western country has suggested the elimination of West Germany as a solution to the German problem. The Conlon Associates recommendation to eliminate the Republic of China, therefore, is neither logical nor legal.[4]

It remains now to examine the views and claims of Communist China and of the Republic of China relative to the legal status of Formosa. The validity of the claims of each government will be examined and objectively presented in an attempt to determine which of the two claimants has right to the title of the island. The views and claims of Communist China are examined first. Then, a brief outline of the rise of Communism in China is described in order to familiarize the reader with the nature of the Communist conspiracy which took place in that country.

[1] *Ibid.*, p. 12.
[2] *Ibid.*, p. 15.
[3] *Ibid.*, p. 16.
[4] *Ibid.*, p. 171-18.

VI. CLAIMS OF THE CHINESE COMMUNISTS

The Chinese Communist victory on the mainland of China was not the result of a short-lived revolution that overthrew the government of Chiang Kai-shek. Rather, it was the culmination of more than 25 years of planning and conspiring between the Soviet Union and the Chinese Communist leaders that finally enabled them to seize control of the government. The success of the Communist revolution can be attributed to several factors. The first of these was the ability of the Communist leaders to form and maintain an army. Although this army suffered many defeats at the hands of the Nationalist forces, it remained intact and was an ever-present threat to the security of the Nationalist Government. The second and perhaps more important factor was the aid which the Chinese Communists received from Russia. It is questionable whether the Chinese Communists could have survived were it not for this assistance.[1]

Russian interference in the domestic affairs of China is of special significance to this study primarily because of the effect it had on the outcome of the revolution. Therefore, the relationship between the Soviet Union and the Chinese Communists must be examined in order to evaluate properly not only Communist China's claim to Formosa but also its right to represent the Chinese people. It should be observed that if the Peiping regime is not the rightful government of China, its claims to Formosa cannot be accepted as valid.

The Soviet relationship with the Chinese Communists is treated in two phases. The first phase deals with the events that took place prior to the end of World War II. The second phase is concerned with the events that took place in China immediately after the war.

In this connection an attempt will be made to show a direct relationship between the Soviet Union and the Chinese Communists and that this relationship was established for the sole purpose of overthrowing the legitimate government of China and establishing a Communist Government dedicated to the ideology of world Communism. The proof of the existence of this relationship will establish the following facts: (1) that a revolutionary conspiracy did, indeed, exist between Moscow

[1] Robert C. North, *Moscow and Chinese Communists*, p. 3 ff.

and the Chinese Communists, and (2) that this conspiracy was an intervention by Russia in the domestic affairs of China.

These two factors will be used as the basis for the examination of the claims of Communist China and the Nationalist Government in this, and in the following chapters of this study.

An exhaustive search for authentic primary sources concerned with the relationship between the Soviet Union and the Chinese Communist leaders has met with moderate success. To those scholars who are familiar with Russia's methods, it should be evident that Russia's foreign policy has always been one of intrigue and deceit. Under such conditions, it is rather difficult to obtain an abundant amount of authentic information on the subject. In discussing the nature of the relationship between the Soviet Union and the Chinese Communists, Robert North commented: Gathering material about Moscow and the Chinese Communists is something like probing in a dark and bottomless pit, and whatever evidence is drawn and put together now, will be subject to new weighing and fresh analyses for years to come. Documents seized in various raids on Soviet diplomatic premises, though bearing every earmark of Communist origin, await systematic appraisal.

It is the firm opinion of the Nationalist Government that the Soviet Union and the Communist Chinese were engaged in a revolutionary conspiracy to subvert and overthrow both the Chinese Government in Peking and the Kuomintang of Dr. Sun Yat-sen.[1] In support of its position, the Chinese Government made public many Russian documents which were seized by Chinese police in several raids on the Soviet Embassy and legation quarters in Peking during April 1927. Some of the documents seized were illegible because they were scorched from an attempted burning.[2] However, from those documents that were salvaged, all but a few have been considered as authentic by scholars familiar with the history of China during the years 1918-1927.[3]

Russia and its Relations with the Chinese Communists before the End of World War II

After World War I, the Chinese Government had hoped to receive assurances from the Allied Powers that its sovereignty and territorial integrity would be respected. It was the wish of the Chinese Government that the Treaty of Versailles would abrogate the unequal treaties

[1] Chiang Kai-shek, *Soviet Russia in China,* 1958, p. 17-19.

[2] David J. Dallin, *The Rise of Russia in Asia,* p. 21-22.

[3] Wilbur, Martin; How, Lien-ying, *Documents on Communism, Nationalism, and Soviet Advisers in China,* 1918-1927, p. 8-37.

which had been forced upon it by these powers. However, the ministers at the Paris Peace Conference were more concerned with the problems of Europe and paid little or no attention to the requests of the Chinese envoys. As a result of this treatment, many intellectuals became embittered with the West and turned to Russia in the hope that Communism would be the answer to the problems of China.

In the early 1920's, two groups emerged, which were to have a most profound effect on the future of China. The first group was the revolutionary government of Dr. Sun Yat-sen known as the Kuomintang. The second group was the small and rather ineffectual Chinese Communist Party. Between these two groups stood the Chinese Government at Peking. This government was the only internationally recognized government of China at that time. However, the authority of the Peking Government was rather impotent and did not extend beyond a limited territorial area.[1] Taking advantage of this, Moscow embarked on its campaign to subvert China to Communism.

Moscow was aware of two important factors. First, the Chinese Communists were not strong enough to wage any large scale campaigns in China. Second, the Kuomintang of Sun Yat-sen was the largest and most powerful revolutionary group in China. Therefore, in order to spread Communism in China, Moscow decided that a coalition of the two parties was necessary. As a result of this decision, the Soviet Union's policy in China followed two basic lines of approach. The first was the infiltrating and subverting of the Kuomintang.[2] The second was supporting and organizing the Chinese Communists in order to establish the Chinese branch of the Comintern.[3]

The Russians first approached Dr. Sun Yat-sen with the idea of a coalition government in 1922. At that time, V. Dalin, the delegate of the Communist Youth League, presented Dr. Sun with a plan for the incorporation of the Communists into the Kuomintang.[4] The idea was flatly rejected by Dr. Sun. However, soon after his conference with Dalin, Dr. Sun met with G. Maring, an official representative of the Cominten. As a result of this meeting, Dr. Sun agreed to accept individual Communists into the Kuomintang as party members with the provisions that:

> no separate cells should exist within the party. The Communists would nonetheless retain the right to continue as a separate party outside the Kuomintang.[5]

[1] David J. Dallin, *The Rise of Soviet Russia in Asia.*, *op. cit.*, p. 204.
[2] Carson Chang, *The Third Force In China*, p. 71.
[3] Carson Chang, *loc. cit.*, p. 71.
[4] Wilbur and How, *op. cit.*, p. 140-141.
[5] Dallin, *The Rise of Soviet Russia in Asia*, *op. cit.*, p. 210.

Following this initial agreement, the Soviet Union sent Adolph Joffe, a special envoy, to meet with Dr. Sun to discuss Chinese-Russian cooperation. Actually Joffe's visit to China had two purposes. The first was to collaborate with the Kuomintang against the Peking Government. The second purpose of his mission was to conclude a formal treaty of recognition with Peking, the very government which Soviet Russia was attempting to overthrow.[1]

The meeting between the two men resulted in the Sun-Joffe Declaration of 1923.[2] The Soviet Union expressed sympathy with the aims of Dr. Sun's revolutionary government, which sought to unify the country and attain national independence. Moreover, Russia assured Dr. Sun that it would support his government and would refrain from interfering in China's affairs.[3]

Dr. Sun was aware of the many dangers involved in an alignment with Moscow. However, he was of the opinion that the Chinese Communists and Russia could be of great help in unifying China.[4] The history of Russian deceit and intrigue in China gives ample evidence that Dr. Sun erred in his judgment of Soviet Russia's intentions in China and of the true nature of the Chinese Communists.[5]

At the same time that Russia pledged to support the Kuomintang, its agents began to carry out the Soviet policy of organizing the Chinese Communists in China. In this connection, Lenin sent Gregori Voitinski to China to organize a Communist movement.[6] Upon his arrival in China, Voitinski learned that a society for the study of Marxism had been established at the University of Peking under the direction of Professor Li-Ta-chao. Taking advantage of a ready-made organization, Voitinski began selecting the best minds among the young intellectuals for the establishment of Communist cells.[7]

In their efforts to subvert the Kuomintang, the Russians encouraged Dr. Sun to establish a central military and political academy. This suggestion was accepted by Dr. Sun, and an academy was established at Whampoa under the direction of Chiang Kai-shek. In his diary Chiang does not mention the directions he received from Soviet agents in organizing the academy. However, the record indicates that:

[1] Chiang Kai-shek, *Soviet Russia in China*, 1958, p. 7.

[2] Hu Shih, "China in Stalin's Grand Strategy," *Foreign Affairs*, October 1950, p. 16-17.

[3] Wilbur and How, *op. cit.*, p. 142-144.

[4] *Ibid.*, p. 138-139.

[5] Chiang Kai-shek, *op. cit.*, p. 26-28.

[6] Wilbur and How, *op. cit.*, p. 138.

[7] Carson Chang, *op. cit.*, p. 69-70.

the dominant role was played by (Michael) Borodin and General Vassili Blucher, who was known in China as Galen.[1]

Further evidence of Soviet participation in the organization of the Whampoa Academy can be seen in a document published under the title, "A Report of the Soviet Secret Agent's Group on the Establishment of the Central Military and Political Academy of the National Revolutionary Army." This report, issued shortly before January 12, 1926, established the objectives of the Academy, the measures to be taken to attain these objectives, the organization of the Academy, the number of students required, the order of replacement and course of study, and, finally, the periods of study and training.[2]

Included in the Soviet Union's conspiracy against the Kuomintang was the training of a number of Chinese officers at the Red Academy in Moscow. At the completion of their training, some of these officers were placed in charge of peasant soviets while others were assigned to the Kuomintang Army.[3] The ultimate role of these Soviet trained officers was to aid in the eventual overthrow of the Kuomintang.[4]

Under the direction of Soviet agents,[5] the Chinese Communists grew in number and in strength.[6] The Chinese Communists were under the complete domination of Moscow from 1923 to 1927. Never before, and never after, was Russian influence so extensive and so intensive as during these three years.[7] During this period, the Soviet Union sent a continuous stream of military men and advisers into China for the sole purpose of subversion.[8] Russia conducted legal and illegal activities simultaneously in order to deceive the Chinese Government and the Kuomintang as to its true intentions.[9] Finally, it was able to establish on Chinese soil a Moscow-directed branch of the Comintern.

So important had Communist activities in China become that Chinese affairs were transferred from the jurisdiction of the foreign office, which had been under the direction of Chicherin, to a special commission of the Politiburo. The real power behind this body was Josef Stalin himself.[10]

[1] Wilbur and How, *op. cit.*, p. 150.
[2] *Ibid.*. Document 18, p. 203-204.
[3] Dallin, *The Rise of Russia in Asia*, *op. cit.*, p. 212.
[4] Robert S. Elegant, *China's Red Masters*, 1951, p. 85-87.
[5] Wilbur and How, Document 22, *op. cit.*, p. 245-247.
[6] General Vo Nguyen Giap, *People's War People's Army*, (tr. by Armed Service Technical Information Agency, Arlington, Virginia), 1955, p. 41B.
[7] Dallin, *The Rise of Russia in Asia*, *op. cit.*, p. 210.
[8] Cheng, Tien-fong, *A History of Sino-Soviet Relations*, p. 121.
[9] Allen S. Whiting, *Soviet Policies in China*, 1917-1924, 1957, p. 35.
[10] Dallin, *The Rise of Russia in Asia*, *op. cit.*, p. 227.

However, during the spring of 1927, Chiang Kai-shek, after a series of incidents with the Chinese Communists, broke with this group and with his Russian advisers. As a result, Chiang became a prime target for Russian agitation. In discussing the relationship between the Chinese Communists and Russia during this period, David Dallin said:

> Ideologically, Moscow was tied up with the bellicose Chinese Communists; Moscow's material help went far beyond ideas and advice. The war of Chinese Communism was Moscow's war. The cause of Chinese Communism was Moscow's war. The cause of Chinese Communism was the cause of a Greater Soviet Union.[1]

After the break with the Kuomintang, Stalin urged the Communist Chinese to form worker and peasant soviets. Stalin was aware that unless the Chinese Communists organized a system of soviets, the Communist cause in China was lost.[2] These soviets would be the nucleus of the future red army. Therefore, in his instructions to the Chinese Communists he advised them that:

> the revolutionary movement could now develop into a Soviet movement in China... Mobilize 20,000 Communists, add some 50,000 revolutionaries... utilize the school's cadets for the officers corps and before it is too late, organize your reliable army.[3]

It should be observed, however, that even after Chiang's break with the Communists, the Soviet Union was willing to make some concessions to him. Soviet policy in this respect was best explained by Stepanov, a Soviet adviser to Chiang, in his report on the "March Twentieth Coup D'Etat." In his report, Stepanov reviewed Chiang's action against the Chinese Communists and the Soviet advisers assigned to Chiang's armies. Stepanov pointed out that in order not to lose everything, it would be better to grant Chiang the concessions he had demanded. In this manner, the Russians could use Chiang's strength and popularity for the cause of the National Revolution. Stepanov concluded his argument by declaring:

> Since our policy is based on utilizing Chiang Kai-shek, the organization of the National (Revolutionary) Army should proceed in accordance with plans already formulated.[4]

The fact that Chiang was no longer willing to cooperate with either the Russians or with the Chinese Communists did not seriously impede the Soviet Union's plans for a Communist revolution in China. Soviet

[1] David Dallin, *Soviet Russia and the Far East*, p. 61.
[2] Wilbur and How, *op. cit.*, p. 403.
[3] David Dallin, *The Rise of Soviet Russia in Asia*, *op. cit.*, p. 230.
[4] Wilbur and How, *op. cit.*, p. 248-253.

agents continued to conspire with the Chinese Communists until the Kuomintang was finally defeated in 1949.

The Soviet emphasis on a strong and independent Chinese Communist Army is what made China's Communists unique compared with those of other Soviet inspired rebellions. Mao Tse-tung was able to recruit the manpower he needed for his Red Army from the peasant soviets. It was this combination, coupled with Russian aid, that led to the defeat of the Kuomintang.[1]

It should be evident from the discussion thus far that a conspiracy did exist between the Soviet Union and the Chinese Communists. An examination of Russia's continuing efforts to subvert and overthrow the Kuomintang is discussed in the following section.

Russia's Interference in the Domestic Affairs of China after World War II

The major difference between the earlier Chinese revolutions—that is, the revolutions of 1911 and 1926 and the Chinese Communist Revolution of 1945-1949 is the fact that the former were nationalistic in nature and origin while the latter was a phase of the Russian revolutionary conspiracy. Evidence of this conspiracy can be seen in the events that have taken place in China since 1945.

Immediately after Russia declared war against Japan in August 1945, the Chinese Communist general, Chu Teh, ordered his army to march into the northern provinces of China. Within a few months the Communist Chinese, disguised as unarmed civilians and Nationalist soldiers, arrived in Manchuria. These troops joined forces with the invading Russians who had brought along with them the Chinese army that had been organized and trained in Russia. With the aid of the Soviet Union, Mao Tse-tung was able to train and supply the Communist armies in the northeast, which were soon to invade China from their bases in Manchuria.[2] In commenting on the Russians' actions in Manchuria, Hu Shih declared:

> Through a most astute and wicked stroke of strategy, Stalin had taken Manchuria and made it the contiguous base for the new military strength of Chinese Communism, behind which lay the unlimited support of Soviet Russia.[3]

Chiang Kai-shek had long recognized the nature of this conspiracy and had fought it for more than twenty years. He also was aware of Russia's threat to peace in Asia as well as to the security of China.

[1] Robert S. Elegant, *op. cit.*, p. 85-87.
[2] David Dallin, *Soviet Russia and the Far East*, *op. cit.*, p. 314.
[3] Hu Shih, *op. cit.*, p. 35-36.

According to the Generalissimo, the Soviet Union considered China the key to the domination of Asia and eventually the world.[1] As early as 1945, the Chinese Government informed the United States that its position in Northern China was precarious and was constantly being endangered by the presence of Russian troops. In a conference with General Marshall, Chow Ching-wen advised him that the Nationalist Government's policy of sending troops to Northern China was doomed to failure because of the interference of the Soviet Union and because of the fact that:

> Even if the Government forces were able to defeat and scatter the Red Army in Chinese uniforms, it would not be possible to defeat the Red Army in Russian uniforms.[2]

It is evident that, as the story of the Chinese Communist victory in China begins to unfold, the conspiracy between the Soviet Union and the Chinese Communist Party becomes more and more clear.

In 1949, the Republic of China, in defending its right to continue to represent the Chinese people in the United Nations, charged the Soviet Union with violations of the Sino-Soviet Treaty of Friendship and Alliance of 14 August 1945 and of the Charter of the United Nations.

In speaking before the General Assembly, Dr. Tingfu Tsiang, the Chinese Representative, pointed out that China and Russia had entered into a treaty in which the Soviet Union had agreed to respect the sovereignty and territorial integrity of China. In addition, the Soviet Union had also agreed to support and assist the Nationalist Government in the postwar reconstruction and rehabilitation of that country. The treaty had stipulated that all Soviet support and assistance would be rendered exclusively to the National Government as the Central Government of China.[3] However, instead of assisting the Nationalist Government as provided for in the treaty, the Soviet Union gave moral and material support to the Chinese Communists.[4]

An example of Soviet aid to the Chinese Communists in direct violation of the Sino-Soviet Treaty of 1945 occurred during November 1946. At that time, Nationalists troops had routed a Communist force of 3000 men. The communist troops crossed the border into North Korea where they were disarmed by the Soviet border guards. How-

[1] Chiang Kai-shek, *op. cit.*, p. 1.
[2] Chow Ching-wen, *Ten Years of Storn*, 1960, p. 18.
[3] Tingfu Tsiang, *Fourth Session of the General Assembly* 230th Plenary Meeting, September 29, 1949, New York, p. 95-97.
[4] Tingfu Tsiang, *Fourth Session of the General Assembly* 272nd Plenary Meeting, December 7, 1949, New York, p. 566-567.

ever, the Chinese Communist troops were quickly transported to the northeast where their weapons were returned and they were allowed to enter Manchuria near Linkiang. This incident could not have taken place without the approval of the Soviet Authorities.[1]

In another incident reported by the Supreme Nationalist Commander in Manchuria, General Hsiung Shih-hui, Soviet gunboats transported Korean troops, technicians, and artillery experts to Shantung province when fighting between the Chinese Communists and Nationalist troops broke out in that area.[2]

The Soviet authorities used every means at their command to hamper and frustrate the Chinese Nationalist Civil Authorities and military commanders in all areas under the control of the Soviet Union.

In continuing the Nationalist Government's charge against the Soviet Union, Ambassador Tsiang declared that his government had long been aware of Russia's imperialistic designs on China. "The Soviet Government," he said, "in addition to the old fashioned methods, had employed a new weapon, namely the creation and support of the Communist Party in China."[3] This Party was completely subservient to the dictates of Moscow. Its primary purpose was to effect the forceful overthrow of the Nationalist Government. In stating his government's position on the Soviet Union's dual policy in Manchuria and in China, Ambassador Tsiang declared:

> That policy was a flagrant violation of the territorial integrity and political independence of a Member State of the Organization and constituted therefore a violation of the United Nations Charter.[4]

In discussing the Soviet's Union relationship with the Chinese Communists after World War II, David Dallin declared:

> Moscow's position in regard to the Chinese Communist regime in Manchuria was one of *de facto* recognition.[5]

It is clear that the actions of the Soviet Union in China both before and after World War II constitute a violation of international law. However, an examination of the Official Records of the United Nations has failed to reveal any indication that the Soviet Union was condemned by that Organization for its acts of aggression in China or for its violation of the Charter of the United Nations or the Sino-Soviet

[1] David Dallin, *Soviet Russia and the Far East, op. cit.*, p. 325.
[2] *Ibid.*, p. 326-327.
[3] Tingfu Tsiang, *Fourth Session of the General Assembly* First Committee, 338th Meeting, November 25, 1949, New York, p. 340.
[4] *Ibid.*, p. 344-345.
[5] David Dallin, *Soviet Russia and the Far East, op. cit.*, p. 331.

Treaty of 1945. It is evident that the United Nations, an organization which was established expressly for the purpose of preventing aggression has by its silence condoned the aggressive policies of Russia in China.

The Legitimacy of the Chinese Communist Government

Russia's interference in the domestic affairs of China has left several areas open to question. The first area is the status or legitimacy of the Chinese Communist Government. Directly related to that question is the validity of the Chinese Communist claims to Formosa. If, as is believed by Russia, Great Britain, and India, the Peiping regime is the legitimate Government of China, then its claims to Formosa are also legitimate. Conversely, if the legal status of the Peiping regime is questionable, then so are its claims to title of the island.

It is significant to note that the China representation question has not been submitted to the International Court of Justice for judicial opinion. For the most part, the member states of the United Nations have been content to discuss the question of Chinese representation in the Security Council and in the General Assembly based on the political aspects rather than on legal principles. Furthermore, both the Chinese Nationalists and the Communists consider the question an internal problem rather than one of international concern.

However, the Chinese Revolution was more than that type of revolution generally accepted to be within the framework of the recognized principles of international law. It cannot be compared with the American or French Revolutions since both of these were nationalistic in nature and scope. The Chinese Revolution was a conspiracy perpetrated on the Chinese people by the Soviet Union and the Chinese Communists. Furthermore, it was intervention in the domestic affairs of a sovereign power by a third state. In the words of Mao Tse-tung, the revolution was world-wide in scope and the interests of the Chinese people were of secondary importance. In commenting on the subject Mao declared:

> The correct thesis that "the Chinese revolution is part of the world revolution" was propounded as early as 1924-1927... It was propounded by the Chinese Communists and approved by all who participated in the Anti-imperialist and anti-feudal stuggles of the time... This correct thesis propounded by the Chinese Communists is based on Stalin's theory.[1]

It is for such reasons as stated by Mao Tse-tung that the Chinese

[1] Mao Tse-tung, "On New Democracy," *The Selected Works of Mao Tse-tung*, Vol. 3, p. 112.

revolution was different from any other before it. It was a revolution which was un-Chinese in nature and in origin. Moreover, participation in the conflict by the Soviet Union has raised the question of a violation of international law. This violation could be the determining factor in the question of Peiping's legitimacy.

In reviewing the works of Starke[1] and Tung,[2] both writers agree that the general rule of international law stipulates that the intervention in the internal affairs of a state by another state is normally prohibited. In discussing the subject of intervention, Hyde observes:

> the fight for the reins of government is not in itself internationally wrongful. Until the conduct of hostilities, by reason of the mode or place of operations, or through some other circumstance, menaces the safety of the outside state, or otherwise directly interferes with the exercise by it of some definite right which should be respected, no ground for intervention is apparent.[3]

There is little question that the Chinese civil war never physically extended beyond the borders of China, nor did it interfere in any manner with the rights of other states. If this line of argument is to be accepted it would appear that the Soviet Union, by aiding the Communist Chinese in the cause of world Communism, has definitely violated international law and that the status of the Peiping regime is questionable.

It should be observed that the Soviet aid to the Communist Chinese is the unprecedented tactics of the International Communist movement—the "Russian Revolutionary Conspiracy." Such tactics are based on secret aid to the dissident elements in a country. These tactics usually encompass deceit, intrigue, and the subversion of the sovereign government both by Soviet agents and by indigenous agents.

However, jurists and writers of international law, such as Hyde,[4] Wilson,[5] Bishop,[6] and Oppenheim,[7] when discussing the subject of intervention in the internal affairs of a state by a third power, are normally referring to open or forcible intervention. Correspondingly, the legal principles of international law relative to intervention have been based on such interpretations.

An example of open intervention in the internal affairs of a state

[1] Joseph G. Starke, *An Introduction to International Law*, p. 89-90.
[2] William L. Tung, *China and Some Phases of International Law*, p. 184.
[3] Charles Cheney Hyde, *International Law, Chiefly as Interpreted and Applied by the United States*, Vol. 1, p. 253.
[4] Hyde, *op. cit.*, p. 254.
[5] George Grafton Wilson, *International Law*, p. 91-98.
[6] William W. Bishop Jr., *International Law, Cases and Materials*, p. 565-567.
[7] L. Oppenheim, *International Law, a Treatise*, (Ed. by H. Lauterpacht, p. 150-151).

occurred during the Spanish Civil war of 1936-1939. So concerned had Great Britain and France become by the armed intervention of Germany, Italy, and Russia in the Spanish conflict, that an international nonintervention agreement was effected by the former countries and eventually agreed upon by 27 states.[1]

The nonintervention scheme was developed outside the League of Nations, and by and large, was excluded from the gaze and consideration of that official body. However, the Spanish Government on several occasions requested the League to set up a system of controls which would render the nonintervention agreement effective.[2] The League usually reacted to the Spanish requests for action by passing mild and ineffective resolutions which supported the nonintervention pact.

However, on October 27, 1937, the League passed a strong resolution on interventions. The resolution stated in part:

> that not merely has the London Nonintervention Committee failed, despite the efforts of the majority of its members... to secure the withdrawal of non-Spanish combatants taking part in the struggle in Spain, but that it must today be recognized that there are veritable foreign Army Corps on Spanish soil, which represent foreign intervention in Spanish affairs.[3]

The efforts of the League were not effective, and the intervening nations continued their aggressions in violation of international law. Such acts of intervention are well-defined and recognizable. However, the intervention of Soviet Russia in the internal affairs of China and other states have always been cloaked in secrecy. Such acts of aggression are not recognized until it is usually too late to save the legally constituted government from defeat at the hands of the Communists.

To date, neither the International Court of Justice nor any other international tribunal has rendered an opinion regarding the revolutionary conspiracy entered into by the Soviet Union and the Communist Chinese. In discussing the conduct of states, Professor Hersch Lauterpacht declared:

> Undoubtedly, it would be more satisfactory if there were an international court endowed with the obligatory jurisdiction to decide questions relating to the conduct of states. But as there is no such obligatory jurisdiction of international tribunals, states themselves are constrained to pronounce judgment upon the legality of the actions of other states.[4]

[1] Norman J. Padeford, "The International Non-Intervention Agreement and the Spanish Civil War," *The American Journal of International Law*, Vol. 31, 1937, p. 595-608.

[2] *Ibid.*, p. 587-589.

[3] P. A. M. Van der Esch, *Prelude to War*, p. 111.

[4] Hersch Lauterpacht, "The Problem of Non-Recognition," *Legal Problems in the Far Eastern Conflict*, by Quincy Wright, p. 135.

The lack of jurisdiction by the International Court of Justice to render its opinions on the conduct of states, specifically on Russian intervention in Chinese affairs, is one of the serious weaknesses of international law. Furthermore, even if the court were empowered to render its opinion in such cases, there is no guarantee that the state that has been charged with committing a wrongful act would abide by the decision of the court. Therefore, in the absence of such opinions by the court, the principles of international law regarding the conduct of states, as now interpreted by the international community, are to be considered applicable to China. Under these circumstances, it appears that Russia's actions in China during the period from 1921 through 1949 were violations of international law.

It is the opinion in some quarters, particularly in the United States and Great Britain, that the Chinese problem has escalated into one of international proportions and, therefore, is the direct concern of the United Nations. During a panel discussion on the subject of foreign intervention in Chinese affairs, Colonel Wade H. Cooper observed that the Communist Government had been in effective control of the Chinese mainland for a number of years and that control would have extended to Formosa had not the United States interfered. Colonel Cooper then asked the members of the panel how such interference on the part of the United States was justified since the Chinese civil war was a domestic matter.[1]

Some members of the panel did not agree with Colonel Cooper's statement. In this connection, Stanley K. Hornbeck pointed out that the conflict in China has never been considered as a civil war in the strict interpretation of that term. According to Mr. Hornbeck:

> the war in China was but one aspect of the international Communist conspiracy, and that the Soviet Union always had been, in fact, a party to this conflict... in view of the nature of Soviet intervention in all Communist inspired revolutions as domestic affairs.[2]

Mr. Hornbeck's argument that the Chinese question is of international concern appears to be questionable, particularly since both parties to the conflict consider it an internal matter. Moreover, the fact that Russia was a party to the Communist revolutionary conspiracy in China does not, in itself, render it a question of international concern

[1] Colonel Wade H. Cooper, "International Law and Current Problems in the Far East," *Proceedings of the American Society of International Law,* April 1955, p. 105.

[2] Stanley K. Hornbeck, "International Law and Current Problems in the Far East," *Proceedings of the American Society of International Law,* April 1955, p. 106.

despite the fact that Russia's actions constituted a violation of International Law.

Closely related to the manner by which the Chinese Communists gained control of the mainland is the method by which they maintain themselves in power. In the opinion of such countries as Great Britain, India, and Russia, the Chinese revolution was over when Chiang Kai-shek and the remnants of his Government fled to Formosa.

However, in the opinion of other nations, particularly the United States, Chiang's flight did not spell the end of the Nationalist Government. The Republic of China continued to function and was still able to carry out its international commitments. The United States was not prepared to recognize the Peiping regime for several reasons, the first of these being that recognition of the Chinese Communists would have meant the withdrawal of recognition from the National Government.[1] The second reason was the fact that the United States was not certain of a Communist China's intentions in the Far East and of its willingness to meet its obligations to its people and to the international community.

However, the Chinese Communists left little doubt as to their intentions toward the international community. In their efforts to establish their control over the populace, the Chinese leaders resorted to the annihilation of all who opposed the new government or its policies. In claiming that Chinese unity had been achieved, Chou En-lai boasted to the All-China Committee of the People's Political Consultative Council that:

> The unprecedented unity of the people has been achieved. More than 2,000,000 bandits have been annihilated in Continental China... with the exception of Formosa... the remnants of counter-revolutionaries have received a severe blow.[2]

As is common in most totalitarian governments, the Communist leaders have denied the Chinese people most of their basic rights. In particular, the Chinese people have been denied the right to vote for a government of their choice. In this respect, it may be noted that the Peiping regime does not meet the test of popular consent[3] which requires that the authority of the new rulers be confirmed by the people.[4] It is evident that the denial of such basic rights, in addition to the

[1] Harvey Cross Dillard, "The Problem of Recognition," *The Yale Review*, Vol. 54, 1954, p. 180.
[2] John Foster Dulles, "Policy For the Far East," United States, *Department of State Bulletin*, No. 1017, Vol. 39, p. 992.
[3] Hyde, *op. cit.*, Vol. 1, p. 161.
[4] Hersch Lauterpacht, *Recognition in International Law*, p. 115.

manner in which the Communist rulers came to power, adds to the questionable status of the government.

China Representation Question and Legal Status of Formosa are Separate but Closely Related Issues

Contrary to popular belief, the China representation question and the legal status of Formosa cannot be considered as one issue. If the Nationalist Government had been able to defeat the Red Chinese, the island would have been formally transferred to that Government in accordance with the provisions of the peace treaty. Similarly, had the Chinese Communists been able to liquidate the Nationalist Government, title of the territory would still have remained with Japan until that Government formally renounced it in the peace treaty.

Today, the Japanese Government no longer holds title to the territory. Furthermore, the question of Chinese representation is still a subject of discussion in the United Nations. Therefore, if it were to be confirmed by the United Nations that Formosa is Chinese territory, the question as to which of the claimant Chinese governments is to be regarded as the rightful one would still have to be solved.[1] It is evident that although the two issues are closely linked they are separate issues and should be treated as such. The Chinese Communists make no distinction between the China representation question and the status of Formosa. As far as Peiping is concerned, it is the rightful government of China and its sovereignty extends to Formosa.

Chinese Communist Position on the Status of Formosa and the Representation Question

The Chinese Communist government made its position on Formosa clear when, in November 1950, it charged the United States with aggression against the island. In appearing before the General Assembly, Mr. Wu Hsiu-Chuan, Special Representative of the Chinese People's Republic, declared:

> Even moderately well-informed people know that Taiwan is an inseparable part of the territory of China... Long before the United States had achieved its independence, Taiwan had already become an inseparable part of the territory of China.[2]

Mr. Wu's statement made it clear that Peiping considers Formosa as its territory and that the United States had intervened in the domestic

[1] Joseph W. Ballantine, Formosa, *A Problem for United States Foreign Policy*, p. 195.

[2] Wu Hsiu-Chuan, "Important Documents Concerning the Question of Taiwan," *Foreign Language Press*, 1959, p. 32.

matters of China. In addition, it is Peiping's belief that all rights to Formosa passed from the Republic of China to the Communist regime by virtue of the Nationalist defeat on the mainland. In continuing his argument, Mr. Wu said:

When the Chinese Government accepted the surrender of the Japanese armed forces in Taiwan, and established sovereignty over the island, Taiwan became, not only *de jure*, but also *de facto*, an inalienable part of Chinese territory... Hence, during the five post war years from 1945 to June 27, 1950, no one ever questioned the fact that Taiwan, *de jure* and *de facto*, is an inseparable part of Chinese territory.[1]

The Communist Chinese hold that Formosa became Chinese Territory through conquest and annexation. According to Peiping, China recovered title to the territory when, in December 1941, it declared war on Japan and unilaterally abrogated the Treaty of Shimonoseki which had ceded the island to Japan in 1895.[2] This argument, which is shared by the Nationalist Government, appears questionable for several reasons. Normally, the common method of regaining lost territory is by obtaining a transfer of title through a treaty of cession.[3] However, Professor Hyde, in discussing the acquisition of territory by conquest, is of the opinion that the victorious state can resort to a different procedure in obtaining title to conquered territory:

The conqueror may formally annex the occupied yet hostile territory to its own domain. By doing so it announces to the outside world both the design to acquire the rights of sovereignty over the area concerned, and the achievement of that end solely by its own act.[4]

Professor Hyde's views are not shared by Fenwick and Bishop who are of the opinion that "the acquisition of title to territory by conquest is technical[5] in nature and is a method rarely[6] used in the present practice of international law." Further, the Chinese Communist argument does not appear to be valid since that government has never exercised control over the island. The argument for conquest and annexation is also weakened by the fact that Japan did not surrender to the Chinese Government alone; it surrendered to the Allied Powers and relinquished *de Facto* control of Formosa to the Nationalist

[1] J. P. Jain, "The Legal Status of Formosa," *The American Journal of International Law*, Vol. 57, No. 1, January 1963, p. 33.
[2] *Ibid.*, p. 34.
[3] Wilson, *op. cit.*, p. 81.
[4] Hyde, *op. cit.*, Vol. I, p. 357.
[5] Charles G. Fenwick, *Cases on International Law*, Chicago, p. 497.
[6] William W. Bishop Jr., *op. cit.*, p. 282.

Government acting in its capacity as a member of the Allied Powers.[1] The Chinese Communist Government was not then, and is not now, considered an Allied Power in that sense of the term.

Moreover, the assertion by the Peiping regime that the unilateral abrogation of the Treaty of Shimonoseki transferred title of Formosa to China appears questionable. Treaties of cession are generally recognized in international law as Executed Treaties. It is the accepted practice in international law that the terms of such treaties are final and cannot be abrogated.[2]

It is evident that China's abrogation of the Treaty of Shimonoseki in 1941 was not a valid act. Therefore, title to Formosa did not pass from Japan to China as a result of that act.

Validity of Communist China's Claims

If the Allied Powers were to confirm that Formosa is an integral part of China, the question of Formosa's sovereignty would still have to be resolved. The Peiping regime's claim to Formosa is contingent to its acceptance as the legitimate government of China. Although Communist China is recognized by many states, it has yet to be admitted into the United Nations in place of the Republic of China. This fact, and the fact that the Chinese Communists were partners with Russia in the revolutionary conspiracy, appear to weaken Peipings' claim to Formosa.

Basically, the Chinese Communists were the direct beneficiaries of illegal acts committed by the Soviet Union in China. It is generally accepted in international law that acts contrary to international law are invalid and cannot become a source of legal rights to the wrongdoer.[3] Interference in the domestic affairs of a state is an act which is contrary to international law.[4] There is no question that the Peiping regime must bear its full share of responsibility for the illegal acts committed against the Nationalist Government. In discussing the consequences of such acts, Professor Lauterpacht declared:

> to admit that... an unlawful act or its consequences and manifestations may become *suo vigore* a source of legal right for the wrongdoer is to introduce into the legal system a contradiction which cannot be solved by a denial of its legal character. International law does not and cannot form an exception to that imperative alternative.[5]

[1] J. P. Jain, *op. cit.*, p. 34.
[2] Charles G. Fenwick, *International Law*, p. 331.
[3] Hersch Lauterpacht, *The Problem of Recognition, op. cit.*, p. 139.
[4] *Cf. infra*, p. 72 ff.
[5] *Ibid.*, p. 140.

If this line of argument is to be accepted it would appear that Peiping's claim to Formosa cannot be considered as valid until the legality of its own status is determined. The question of the legality of the Communist Government is discussed in Chapter VII of this work.[1] Conversely, if it is confirmed that the Chinese Communists did not commit any unlawful acts in assuming control of the Chinese mainland, it would appear that the status of the Republic of China is indeed questionable. It remains, therefore, to examine the claims of the Nationalist Government and to establish, if possible, the legal status of Formosa in light of the arguments presented by that Government.

[1] *Cf. infra*, p. 74 ff.

VII. CLAIMS OF THE REPUBLIC OF CHINA

The question of Formosa's sovereignty cannot be solved from a legal point of view until several basic determinations have been made. First, and most important to this study, is whether or not it can be proven that Formosa is an integral part of China. If so, then it must be determined which of the claimant entities is the rightful government. Closely related to the latter issue is the question of the state of hostilities between the rival factions. Therefore, if it can be said that the conflict in China is a civil war that has not yet reached its conclusion, it would appear that the claims of the Republic of China are legitimate. Under these circumstances, the international character of the Peiping regime would indeed be questionable. Assuming that this argument is correct, the conflict would then be considered an internal Chinese matter. It follows then that intervention in this conflict by third parties would be considered a violation of international law. However, the same set of circumstances would give the Chinese Communists the right to attempt to seize Formosa without interference from third parties.[1]

But if Formosa is not Chinese territory, as is claimed by Great Britain and the United States neither the Nationalist Government nor the Peiping regime can claim title to the island. The Nationalist Government would then be considered as a government in exile occupying disputed territory. Yet as an Allied Power and as a signatory to the Instrument of Surrender, it appears that the Republic of China could enter into a treaty of cession with the Japanese Government. The fact that the Republic of China was not a signatory to the San Francisco Peace Treaty should not be considered a deterring factor in the event that these governments decided to effect such an agreement. As a matter of fact, the Japanese Government, recognizing the legal status of the Republic of China, entered into a separate treaty of peace with that Government on 28 April 1952. Although the treaty did not cede Formosa to the Nationalist Government, it terminated the state of war which had existed between the two Governments. If a treaty of

[1] Li Thian-hok, "The China Impasse," *Foreign Affairs*, April 1958, Vol. 36, p. 437.

peace between Japan and the Republic of China is considered valid, then it is evident that a treaty of cession would also be acceptable.

Nationalist Government is the Legitimate Government of China

None of the proposals examined thus far appear to offer a legally valid solution to the Formosan question. The most significant factor which has militated against such a solution is the continued existence of the Republic of China. Although many nations have extended recognition to the Chinese Communists, the Nationalist Government is still recognized by an absolute majority of the member states of the United Nations.[1] Moreover, it has continued to function as a sovereign state and has been able to discharge its international obligations.

As a result of its participation in the San Francisco Conference of 1945, the Republic of China became one of the original members of the United Nations. It has since held and continues to hold a permanent seat in the Security Council. There appears little question that the Nationalist Government is entitled to its seat in the United Nations since it has met the requirements of Article 3 of the Charter which specified:

> The original members of the United Nations shall be the States which, having participated in the United Nations Conference on International Organizations at San Francisco, or having previously signed the Declaration by the United Nations of January 1, 1942, sign the present Charter and ratify it in accordance with Article 110.[2]

However, the conditions of Article 3 have been disregarded by such States as Russia, India, and Pakistan in their attempt to unseat the Nationalist Government in favor of Peiping. In discussing the subject before the General Assembly, Sir Zafrulla Khan, the Pakistani Representative declared:

> China is not applying for membership of the United Nations. It is a member-state, a permanent member of the Security Council, one of the Big Five.[3]

In this instance, Ambassador Khan is referring to the Central Peoples Republic of China whose cause he was espousing in the United Nations. However, it is a matter of history that the Peiping regime did not participate in the San Francisco Conference since it was not in existence at that time. Further, the Chinese member of the "Big Five" referred to

[1] Adlai E. Stevenson, "Albanian Proposal to Change United Nations Representation of China Rejected," *Department of State Bulletin*, No. 1272, Vol. 79, No. 11, 1963, p. 755.

[2] United Nations, *Charter of the United Nations*, Article 3, August 1945, p. 9.

[3] Mohamed Samin Khan, "Legal Aspects of the Problem of China's Representation in the United Nations," *Pakistan Horizon*, Vol. 10, No. 3, September 1957, p. 140.

in this speech is the Republic of China. Under these circumstances it is evident that Ambassador Khan's argument for Peiping is not legally valid since it does not meet the requirements of Article 3 of the United Nations Charter.[1]

In refuting such statements and in answer to the Soviet Union's request to the General Assembly that it refuse to recognize the credentials of the Republic of China, Ambassador Tsiang declared:

> the Government which I have the honor to represent was one of the founders of this Organization and one of the Authors of the Charter. The Charter of the United Nations specified that the Republic of China should be one of the five permanent members of the Security Council. We are here because we represent the Chinese people and because the Charter gives us that right.[2]

It is evident that Ambassador Tsiang's argument in defending his government's right to represent China in the United Nations is correct. The Ambassador has made it clear that his government's claims are based on legal rights and are guaranteed by the Charter. To deny the Nationalist Government its rightful place in the Security Council would be to deny the legal binding effect of the Charter upon the signatories to that document. It follows, therefore, that the Formosan issue involves the right of a sovereign government to continue in existence even after it has lost a major portion of its territory. Furthermore, it involves the right of that government to lay claim to title of the territory it occupies and which is claimed by the rival government.

Succession of Governments

The transfer of the seat of the Nationalist Government to Formosa did not, in itself, signify the end of that government; nor did the move divest the Nationalist Government of its sovereign rights. The move was viewed by Chiang Kai-shek as a shift to a new base of operations from which his Government could continue its fight against the Communists.[3] It is evident that if the Chinese Communists had been successful in liquidating the Nationalist Government, the question of Formosa's status would not be a subject of controversy today. The Allied Powers would have treated the conflict as an internal problem and in all probability the issue would have been considered closed. However, the question of Formosa's legal status remains the subject

[1] *Cf. supra*, p. 69.
[2] Tingfu F. Tsiang, United Nations, *Official Records of the General Assembly*, Eleventh Session, 658 Plenary Meeting, February 21, 1957, p. 1187.
[3] Chiang Kai-shek, "President Chiang Reviews World Situation," *Statement at Conference of High Government Officials*, Taipei, February 8, 1955, p. 1.

of bitter controversy between the claimant entities. Both Taipei and Peiping have claimed title to the island on the basis that it is an integral part of China.

If it is accepted that Formosa is part of Chinese territory, then it would appear that the territory the Nationalist Government is in, is a portion of its own territory. Under these circumstances it can be said that the continuity of that Government was not broken as a result of its move to the island. The Nationalist Government cannot be considered a government in exile, as was Free France during World War II.

Although it is evident that some of its activities have been curtailed by the Communist rebellion, the executive, judicial, and legislative bodies of the Nationalist Government have continued to function according to law. Moreover, the activities of the provincial and Hsien governments have continuously increased their functions as prescribed by the constitution.[1]

It appears, therefore, that the rival entity that has emerged in China as a result of a revolution claims to be the legal government of that nation. This entity seeks to succeed the existing Government of Chiang Kai-shek on the basis that his government does not represent the Chinese people and that it is in illegal possession of Chinese territory.

Red China's claims to legitimacy and to Formosa's sovereignty have created many problems in the interpretation and application of the doctrine of recognition. As has been evident in the case of China, most states have treated the question from a political rather than a legal viewpoint. In summing up the reasons for this approach to the doctrine of recognition by the various states, Professor Lauterpacht commented:

> there is probably no other subject in the field of international relations in which law and politics appear to be more closely interwoven. As a result, there has grown up a tendency to maintain that the crucial question of granting or refusing recognition is not one of international law.[2]

Normally, a change of government conducted in a normal and constitutional manner would create no problem in international law. For example, there is no need for an expressed act of recognition by third states when, after an election in the United States or in Great Britain, the victorious party assumes control of the government. In such instances there is no question of the creation of a new personality.[3] The

[1] Republic of China, *The Constitution of the Republic of China*, Chapter XI, p. 17-19.
[2] Hersch Lauterpacht, *Recognition in International Law*, preface, p. iv.
[3] Charles Cheney Hyde, *International Law, Chiefly as Interpreted and Applied by the United States*, p. 159-160.

personality belongs to the state and necessarily survives the change of government.

However, when the new government assumes power through revolution, third states usually withhold recognition until the situation becomes clarified.[1] It is evident that the legitimacy of such a government would be questionable since it did not assume control through constitutional means. A prime example of this type of government is the Chinese Communist regime now in control of the Chinese mainland. In a discussion on the subject of recognition, Professor Chen Ti-chiang reviewed the doctrine of legitimacy or constitutionalism. According to Professor Chen Ti-chiang, this doctrine maintains that:

> every government that comes to power in a country depends for its legality, not upon mere *de facto* possession, but upon its compliance with the established legal order of that country.[2]

The United States and Great Britain have, from time to time, resorted to the doctrine of legitimacy when it suited a particular need. However, it has been the practice of some states[3] to disregard the manner by which a government has assumed power. According to these states, the fact that the government is in possession of the territory and its people and the fact that its tenure is reasonably assured is sufficient reason for recognition. As applied to China, the doctrine of legitimacy appear to be valid since the Chinese Communists in assuming control of the mainland violated Article 139 of the Constitution which states:

> No political party and no individual shall make use of armed force as in instrument in a struggle for political power.[4]

There is little question that the Chinese Communists acted in defiance of the constitution and in violation of the laws of China. The Nationalist Government, therefore, has the right, under Chinese Law, to declare the Peiping regime an illegal and treasonable government. Under such circumstances, the Republic of China has the right to use every means at its command to expel the rebel government from its control of the mainland.

The question of two entities claiming to represent China in the United Nations was discussed in the General Assembly early in 1950. After some deliberation of the issues involved, that body declared:

[1] Chen Ti-Chiang, *The International Law of Recognition*, p. 105.
[2] *Ibid.*, p. 108.
[3] Charles G. Fenwick, *International Law*, D. Appleton, 1934, p. 118-120.
[4] *The Constitution of the Republic of China*, *op. cit.*, Chapter XIII, p. 20.

that in cases of that description, the question should be considered in the light of the Purposes and Principles of the Charter and the circumstances of each case.[1]

It is evident that the General Assembly merely considered the existence of two authorities claiming to represent China. That body did not consider the effect of the doctrine of legitimacy on the legality of the Peiping regime, nor was there a study made on Chinese Communist violations of the Constitution of China. Furthermore, the General Assembly did not consider the right of the Republic of China to continue to represent its people in the United Nations and it did not consider the Nationalist Government's right to remain in occupation of Formosa. The General Assembly's failure to take definite action on the China question left open the possibility of Communist China's entry into the United Nations at a future date.

Succession of States

As discussed earlier, the two-China concept has been found unacceptable by both Taipei and Peiping. An examination of this concept has revealed several areas that appear questionable when viewed from the standpoint of international law. Both entities could be said to satisfy the conditions of statehood since each has a people, a defined territory, and a sovereign government.[2] The question then becomes, which of the claimant entities would be recognized as the legal government of China? Assuming that Communist China is recognized as the legal government of China, the question of Formosa's status would not be automatically settled. First, it would have to be determined whether the island is Chinese territory. If this were confirmed, Communist China could not claim title to Formosa since the territory has not been ceded to it nor has it ever held possession of the island. The Republic of China would no longer represent China and would be known as the Republic of Formosa. Under these conditions the island could be ceded to the new republic by the Allied Powers after it was recognized as a new state. It follows, then, that a new state could be created by applying the principle of succession of states. However, a state cannot be created from a territory which does not wish to relinquish its claim to represent the Chinese people. The Republic of China obviously intends to maintain this position indefinitely.

[1] L. Oppenheim, (Ed. by H. Lauterpacht), Vol. 2, *op. cit.*, p. 134.
[2] Chen Ti-chiang, *op. cit.*, p. 55-62.

The Republic of China has never extended Recognition to the Chinese Communists in any Form

Civil wars and revolutions, if successful or partially successful, inevitably raise issues about the recognition of governments and states. However, prior to extending recognition to a rebel government, there is a period during the conflict when the parent state would, for legal or humane reasons, recognize the belligerency of the insurgents.

In the Chinese revolution, the Nationalist Government, recognizing the nature of the Communist conspiracy, never recognized the belligerency of the Chinese Communists. The Nationalist policy of nonrecognition was guided by both political and legal considerations. In the first instance, the very nature of the conflict dictated against such recognition since the Communists conducted a guerilla-type war from hidden bases in the Chinese hills. The Chinese Red Army never launched any major attacks against the Nationalist troops. It was a conflict fought over a 20-year period in which the Communist guerillas harassed the Nationalist forces and then retreated in the face of offensives launched by the government. According to Mao Tse-tung these tactics were designed to wear down, frustrate, and demoralize the Nationalist troops.[1]

Under such unorthodox conditions of warfare, the Nationalist Government was correct in not recognizing the belligerency of the Communists. In addition, the conflict was of such a nature that third states could recognize neither the insurgency or belligerency of the Chinese Communists. To have done so would have been an affront to the Republic of China and a violation of international law.[2]

In the second instance, it is a general practice among nations that the parent state ramely accords such recognition to insurgents.

While international lawyers are not in complete agreement on the legal status of belligerency,[3] it is noteworthy to observe the position taken by Ti-Chiang chen:

> A belligerent body, properly organized, is capable of exercising rights and fulfilling duties under international law in substantially the same manner as a sovereign state in so far as concerns the prosecution of the war, although it does not constitute a state, nor is it entitled to represent the state internationally.[4]

[1] Mao Tse-tung, "Characteristics of China's Revolutionary War" Vol. I, 1955, *The Selected Works of Mao Tse-tung*, p. 195.

[2] Georg Schwarzenberger, *A Manual of International Law*, Vol. 1, p. 70.

[3] See L. Oppenheim, *International Law, a Treatise*, (Ed. by H. Lauterpacht), Vol. 2, p. 248.

[4] Ti-chiang chen, *op. cit.*, p. 306.

The controversial question of recognition is contingent upon various factors. However, it is generally accepted in international law that several conditions must be satisfied prior to the recognition of belligerency by either the parent state or by third parties. The first of these conditions is that a state of hostilities is in existence and is being carried on by two political bodies.[1] A second condition is that the insurgent group must exercise a *de facto* control over persons and territory within the limits of the state being contested.[2] Another condition of belligerency requires that the insurgents command an army, which is prepared to exercise the rules of warfare.[3] A fourth condition imposed on insurgents is that the group must act under the direction of a ressponsible authority.[4] Finally, there is the practical necessity for third states to define their attitude to the conflict.[5]

The last condition is of significance in the case of China. In addition to the recognition of belligerency being withheld by the Nationalists, no nation extended recognition to the Chinese Communists until after the Nationalist defeat on the mainland. As discussed earlier, the only nation that aided the Chinese Communists was Russia. That the Soviet act was a violation of international law is without question. In discussing the subject of aid to insurgents, Professor Hyde declared:

> any aid or recognition accorded to an insurgent, or revolutionary body, which is incapable of assuming the conditions required for the recognition of belligerency, is considered intervention in the affairs of the parent state.[6]

The Chinese Communists did not meet the conditions of belligerency particularly during the period 1928 through 1937. It was only after the Japanese invasion of China in 1937 and the entry of the United States into World War II in 1941 that the revolutionaries were able to gain the military strength to harass the Nationalist Government. Furthermore, China's preoccupation in the war with Japan played a secondary but important role in the emergence of the Chinese Communists. In view of what has been discussed thus far, the Nationalist Government's policy of nonrecognition of belligerency appears to have been correct.

[1] L. Oppenheim, (Ed. by H. Lauterpacht), Vol. 2, *op. cit.*, p. 249.
[2] William Bishop Jr., *International Law*, p. 264.
[3] Fenwick, *op. cit.*, p. 112.
[4] Charles Cheney Hyde, *International Law*, Vol. 3, p. 1792.
[5] George Grafton Wilson, *Handbook of International Law*, p. 47.
[6] Hyde, *op. cit.*, Vol. 1, p. 201.

State of Hostilities still exists

International law does not stipulate the precise moment at which recognition may be extended to a new government or state. This is a judgement that must be made solely by the state granting recognition. In the case of revolutions, recognition of the belligerent community is normally withheld by third parties until the belligerents are recognized by the parent state, and, when a third party accords recognition to a belligerent community before it is recognized by the parent state, such recognition is considered premature. The parent state usually considers premature recognition as an offensive act amounting, in some cases, to an act of intervention.

The Republic of China has always considered the recognition of the Peiping regime as an act of intervention by such states as Russia, Great Britain, India, and France. In all instances, the Nationalist Government's reply to these acts has been the severance of diplomatic relations with the offending nation. These governments have based recognition of Peiping on the premise that it is in *de facto* control of the mainland. However, the Republic of China has insisted that *de facto* control of territory by a belligerent community is not, in itself, sufficient grounds for recognition. According to the Nationalist Government, the Communist revolutionaries are not Chinese. Furthermore, the revolt cannot be considered nationalistic in nature or origin since it was part of the Communist revolutionary conspiracy. In stating his Government's position on the question, Ambassador Tsiang declared:

> Those Communists in my country are not Chinese; Communism is un-Chinese in origin, un-Chinese in purpose and character.[1]

Based on this argument, the Nationalist Government has remained adamant in its attitude toward any possible conciliation with the Peiping regime. Thus, the Nationalist Government does not consider the revolution as concluded. The Nationalist claims appear valid since there has never been a cease-fire agreement, an armistice, or a treaty of peace effected between the two rivals. The struggle continues through bombardments, commando raids, and propaganda. Insofar as the Republic of China is concerned, the conditions of war, which have existed since 1928, continue to exist today. In commenting on the acquisition of territory, Professor Ti Chiang-chen said:

[1] Ambassador Tingfu Tsiang, United Nations, *General Assembly, Official Records,* Eleventh Session, 658th Plenary Meeting, February 21, 1957, p. 1187.

war creates a temporary state of things. The occupation of the territory by the army does not confer title upon the occupant. The occupied territory, although for the time being beyond the actual control of the legitimate sovereign, may still be considered as constructively under his sovereignty.[1]

An interesting parallel to the Chinese Representation question can be drawn from the Italo-Ethiopian war of 1936. After the Italian forces had captured Addis Ababa, Italy decreed the annexation of Ethiopia on May 9, 1936. However, Ethiopia's right to membership in the League of Nations and its right to be represented at League meetings was upheld on the grounds that the Italian troops were not in complete control of Ethiopian territory. It was the opinion of the League members that the extinction of the Ethiopian State was not conclusively established.[2] If this argument is accepted, then the same principles of international law that applied to Ethiopia in 1936 should apply to the Republic of China today.[3]

If the Nationalist Government's claim that the revolution has not ended is confirmed, it appears that recognition of Peiping has been premature. It is generally accepted that international law does not consider revolutions as unlawful. However, international law does not make a distinction between the belligerent community and the parent state. In discussing the recognition of the belligerent community by third states, Professor Lauterpacht declared:

So long as the revolution has not been fully successful, and so long as the lawful government, however adversely affected by the fortunes of the civil war, remains within the national territory, and asserts its authority, it is presumed to represent the State as a whole.[4]

International law recognizes two modes of termination of war: treaties of peace and subjugation. However, at times, simple cessation of all acts of war on the part of the warring factions has brought hostilities to an end. This latter method, however, does not formally bring the state of war to an end.[5]

Since both Peiping and Taipei agree that a state of hostilities continues in existence and since war creates a temporary state of things, it appears that the Nationalist claims are valid. Under these conditions,

[1] Chen Ti-Chiang, *op. cit.*, p. 63.
[2] *Ibid.*, p. 64-65.
[3] Richard Harvey, "The Legal Status of Formosa," *World Affairs Quarterly*, Vol. 30, 1959-1960, p. 149.
[4] Hersch Lauterpacht, *Recognition in International Law*, p. 93.
[5] Oppenheim, *International Law, a Treatise*, Vol. 2 (Ed. by H. Lauterpacht), p. 497-599.

the Republic of China "is entitled to continued recognition *de jure* so long as the civil war, whatever its prospects, is still in progress.[1]

San Francisco Treaty of Peace

The signing and ratification of the Peace Treaty on April 28, 1952 formally terminated the war between Japan and the Allied Powers. The treaty was to be the vehicle for the settlement of the territorial claims of the Allied Powers against Japan. Among these claims was the restoration of Formosa to the Republic of China.

However, at the time of the Peace Conference the right of the Republic of China to represent the Chinese people was disputed by the Chinese Communists. The Communist claims were supported by the Soviet Union and Great Britain, and, as a result, the Allied Powers disagreed on which of the claimants should be seated at the conference. The question was settled by allowing neither the Republic of China nor the Peiping regime to attend the conference or become signatories to the treaty. The decision, while appearing to be just, was merely an appeasement of the Chinese Communists since it denied the Republic of China its legal right to be seated at the conference.

The ratification of the treaty and its coming into force did not settle the question of Formosa's legal status for several reasons. In the first instance, Japan merely renounced all right title and claim to the territory. Second, there was no expressed cession of the island either to China, or to any of the Allied Powers. It should be observed that the only effect the treaty had on the status of Formosa, was that Japan had formally renounced its sovereignty over the island. This renunciation could in no way be construed as a declaration of cession. Under such conditions, title of Formosa would not have passed from Japan to the Nationalist Government even if the latter had been a signatory to the treaty.

Studying the treaty reveals that there were no provisions made for the future of any of the territories Japan lost as a result of the war. In particular, Article 2 of the treaty was not quite clear on the status of Formosa; the status of the island remained undetermined simply because the Allied Powers could not agree on its ultimate disposition.[2] The underlying reason for this indecision was the fact that some of the participants at the conference had recognized Red China and did not want to risk offending that government. It was decided, therefore, that

[1] Lauterpacht, *op. cit.*, p. 94.

[2] D. P. O'Connell, "The Status of Formosa and the Chinese Recognition Problem," *The American Journal of International Law*, Vol. 50, April 1956, p. 406.

the question of Formosa's status would be discussed at a future date.

The terms of the treaty and the manner in which it was written leaves that document open to interpretation where the rights of China are concerned. Article 21 states:

Notwithstanding the provisions of Article 25 of the present treaty, China shall be entitled to the benefits of Articles 10 and 14 (a) 2.[1]

In accordance with the provisions of Article 10, Japan renounced all special rights and interests in China.[2] Article 14(a) 2 gave China the right as an Allied Power, in addition to receiving reparations, to liquidate or retain all property, rights, and interests of Japan.[3]

There are several matters of legal interest in the three Articles referred to above. First, all reference to the Republic of China has been deleted. In its place has been substituted the word "China." The implication in this instance is that China could mean the Republic of China or the Central People's Republic of China. The deliberate omission of all reference to the Republic of China by the states participating in the drafting of the treaty is an offensive act directed against a sovereign government. Furthermore, it has given the supporters of the Peiping regime an effective point of argument when defending the cause of Communist China. The usual retort by such groups is that the treaty does not specify which China is legally entitled to exercise its rights under the terms of that document.

The second point of legal interest is the special provisions in Articles 10, 14 (a) 2 and 21 in connection with Chinese rights guaranteed by the treaty. These provisions were granted to China despite the fact that the Republic of China was not a signatory to the treaty. It is to be observed that the legal significance of the stipulated provisions is questionable. However, "It is possible that Japan's renunciation of its right in China confers at least an interest in that state which could be internationally asserted by it."[4]

An examination of Article 25 indicates that the Peiping regime is not considered an Allied Power and cannot derive any benefits from the provisions of the treaty. In this connection, Article 25 specifies in part:

[1] United States, Department of State, *Treaty of Peace With Japan*, Pub. 4613, Series 2490 April 1952 p. 22.

[2] *Ibid.*, p. 11.

[3] *Ibid.*, p. 14-16.

D. P. O'Connell, "Legal Aspects of the Peace Treaty With Japan," *The British Year Book of International Law*, Vol. 29, (Ed. by E. Lauterpacht), 1953, p. 428.

For the purposes of the present treaty, the Allied Powers shall be the states at war with Japan... Subject to the provisions of Article 21, the present treaty shall not confer any rights, titles or benefits on any state which is not an Allied Power as herein defined.[1]

There can be no lawyers' doubts as to the right of the Republic of China to qualify as an Allied Power under the provisions of Article 25. Until April 28, 1952, when a peace treaty was signed between Japan and the Republic of China, a state of war continued to exist between the two countries. Moreover, there is no evidence that a state of hostilities exists, or has existed, between the Central People's Republic of China and Japan. In view of these facts, it is not clear how the Allied Powers had the legal right to deny the Republic of China its seat at the conference table.

The Allied Powers, aware that China and Japan were still at war, provided the legal means in Article 26 by which the two countries could end the state of war existing between them. Article 26 provided that:

Japan will be prepared to conclude with any state which signed or adhered to the United Nations declaration of January 1, 1942, and which is at war with Japan, or with a state which previously formed a part of the territory of a state named in Article 23, which is not a signatory of the present treaty, a bilateral Treaty of Peace on the same or substantially the same terms as are provided for in the present treaty. [2]

It should be observed that the terms of the Article specifically excluded the Central People's Republic of China as one of the states with which Japan could sign a Treaty of Peace. In the first instance, the Peiping regime was not a signatory to the United Nations Declaration of January 1, 1942. Secondly, since hostilities between Japan and the Allied Powers formally ceased on September 2, 1945, it should be evident, that Peiping and Japan have never been at war. Finally, the Central People's Republic of China, or "China," is not one of the nations referred to in Article 23 of the treaty.[3] The reference to this section in Article 25 was to permit Japan to conclude peace treaties with nations that were at one time territories of the Allied Powers.

It is clear, therefore, that although the treaty refers only to "China," that "China" referred to is unmistakably the Republic of China. The decision by the Allied Powers to exclude the Nationalist Government from participating in the Peace Conference was based on political

[1] Treaty of Peace with Japan, *op. cit.*, p. 24.
[2] Treaty of Peace with Japan, *loc. cit.*, p. 24.
[3] *Ibid.*, p. 23.

factors rather than on legal principles. The Republic of China was excluded from becoming a signatory to the Peace Treaty by the very powers that agreed to restore Formosa to it at Cairo. This act by Great Britain and the Soviet Union has delayed the retrocession of the island to the Republic of China.

Sino-Japanese Treaty of April 28, 1952

The Japanese Government showed little interest in effecting a bilateral treaty with the Republic of China as provided for in Article 26 of the San Francisco Treaty. However, after a series of discussions with State Department officials, the Japanese Government finally declared its intentions. In a letter to Ambassador Dulles, Premier Yoshida advised the Ambassador that Japan was prepared to conclude a treaty of peace with the Republic of China, and thereby establish normal relations between the two Governments. In connection with the proposed treaty, Premier Yoshida said:

> The terms of such a bilateral treaty shall, in respect to the Republic of China, be applicable to all territories which are now, or which may hereafter be, under the control of the National Government of China.[1]

The Sino-Japanese Peace Treaty was signed at Taipei, Formosa, on April 28, 1952. The treaty was similar in many respects to the San Francisco Treaty. The Protocol of the Treaty, signed on the same day, reiterated some of the conditions of the San Francisco Treaty, and declared the terms of Chapter V, Articles 14 (a) and 18 referring to "claims and property" not applicable to Japan.[2] Article I of the treaty formally terminated the state of war which had existed between the Republic of China and Japan.

Article II reiterated the provisions of Article 2 of the San Francisco Treaty in which, "Japan has renounced all right, title, and claim to Taiwan..."[3]

By the terms of Article 2 of the San Francisco Treaty, Formosa formally became derelict while under the *de facto* control and administration of the Nationalist Government. There has been no explanation from either signatory as to the reason why the island was not formally retroceded to the Republic of China at that time. There appears to be little doubt that Japan had the legal right to cede the territory to the

[1] Shigeru Yoshida, "Japan's Future Policy Toward China," *Department of State Bulletin*, Vol. 26, No. 657, January 28, 1952, p. 120.

[2] Republic of China, *Treaty of Peace Between the Republic of China and Japan*, April 28, 1952, p. 5.

[3] *Ibid.*, p. 1.

Nationalist Government. Moreover, the Republic of China, as an Allied Power, had the right to enter into such an agreement despite the fact that its Allies did not see fit to fulfill the obligations of the Cairo Declaration. A bilateral treaty, once ratified by the signatories, is a legal document and its provisions shall be binding upon the parties to the agreement. It follows that the protestations of other states should not affect the legal character of such a transaction. However, since the territory was not formally retroceded to the Republic of China, the provisions of Article II cannot be construed as having transferred title of the island from Japan to the Nationalist Government.

Furthermore, examination of the treaty revealed several other Articles that are of special interest to this study. In accordance with the provisions of Article IV:

All treaties, conventions, and agreements concluded before December 9, 1941, between China and Japan have become null and void as a consequence of the war.[1]

The assumption in this instance is that the definition of "all treaties" in this article also includes the Treaty of Shimonoseki in which China ceded Formosa to Japan. However, without an expressed act of cession, it cannot be said that the provisions of Article IV have transferred title of the island from Japan to the Republic of China. Moreover, the Japanese Government has remained silent in connection with the legal effect of Article IV on the status of Formosa.

Article X is also of special interest since it deals with the nationality of the Formosans and of persons who come under the jurisdiction of the Republic of China. In accordance with its provisions and for the purposes of the treaty:

nationals of the Republic of China shall be deemed to include all the inhabitants and former inhabitants of Taiwan.[2]

Thus, Japan, without formally ceding Formosa to the Nationalist Government, has recognized the fact that the Formosans are once again Chinese citizens. As such, they are subject to the laws and regulations of the Republic of China. However, the validity of the provisions of Article X appears to be questionable for several reasons. First, one of the accepted modes of acquiring nationality is by cession of territory. In discussing the question of nationality Professor Oppenheim said,

[1] *Ibid.*, p. 2.
[2] *Ibid.*, p. 3.

"the inhabitants of the ceded territory acquire, *ipso facto* by the cession, the nationality of the state which acquires the territory."[1]

If this argument is to be accepted, then it must be assumed that the Formosans became Japanese subjects after the island was ceded to Japan in 1895. It follows then that the Formosans were no longer considered Japanese subjects at the time Japan renounced title to the island in April 1952. Under these circumstances, it is not clear how the nationality of the Formosans could be transferred from Japan to China without a treaty of cession being concluded. That is, unless the provisions of Article IV are to be considered as tacit recognition by Japan that the sovereignty of Formosa has been transferred to the Republic of China.

By the ratification of the Sino-Japanese Treaty of 1952, Japan served notice to the United Nations that the state of hostilities between the two nations had ceased. In addition, the Japanese Government formally declared that it had recognized the Republic of China as the legitimate representative of the Chinese people in the United Nations. Japan is also aware that the Nationalist Government still maintains actual authority over certain territory, meaning, of course, Formosa, the Pescadores and some of the coastal islands of China.[2]

The legal effect of the Sino-Japanese Treaty on the status of Formosa is questionable. The Japanese Government having recognized the Republic of China and having concluded a Treaty of Peace with it, does not in itself settle the question of Formosa's sovereignty.

Nationalist Government's Views on Status of Formosa

One of the more important issues in the Formosan problem is whether or not the conflict in China is an internal affair. If the conflict is an internal Chinese matter, then the dispute between Peiping and Taipei represents a civil war. Under these conditions, any attempt by third states to obstruct Chiang Kai-shek in attacking the mainland can be construed as interference in the domestic affairs of China.

The United States has taken the position, along with Great Britain, that the struggle in China is not an internal affair of the Chinese people. Ely Maurer points out that it cannot be classified merely as a civil war since Russia, in violation of its treaty with the Republic of China, aided the Chinese Communists by supplying them with arms and equipment during the rebellion. This Russian aid to the Chinese Com-

[1] Oppenheim, Vol. 1, *op. cit.*, p. 656-657.
[2] Shigeru Yoshida, *op. cit.*, p. 121.

munists was instrumental in the defeat of the Nationalist forces.[1] Maurer's views are shared by Professor Quincy Wright who, in commenting on the Formosa question, observed:

> According to the Stimson doctrine there is a duty not to recognize a new state or other territorial change established, not primarily by internal action, but by the aggression of another state in violation of international obligations.[2]

It is the opinion of Professor Wright that even though the revolutionaries are aided by third parties, the change in government is primarily in the constitutional, not in the international, order. In addition, international law favors recognition of a general *de facto* government. Such a government is considered competent, even though it is not generally recognized. However, according to Professor Wright, "the situation is different if the outside aid is so extensive that it results in making the revolutionary government a satellite of its benefactor."[3]

To those familiar with the revolutionary conspiracy, it was evident that Russia had intended China to be subservient to its wishes. To Russia, China was the first step in the communization of Asia. However, its intervention in China's domestic affairs cannot be considered international in scope despite the fact that its goal is a Communist world.

The arguments presented by Ely Maurer and by Professor Wright are not shared by either Chiang Kai-shek or Mao Tse-tung. Both leaders are of the opinion that the entire China question, including the China representation question and the legal status of Formosa, is an internal matter. In the opinion of Chiang Kai-shek, his Government is not occupying foreign territory but a portion of Chinese territory. Pursuing this line of argument, the generalissimo contends that the conflict is not the concern of third states but of the Chinese people. His argument is based on the premise that Formosa became Chinese territory after the Japanese surrender. In discussing the status of Formosa, President Chiang declared:

> When Japan surrendered, the Government of the Republic of China repossessed Taiwan and Penghu... Since that time Taiwan and Penghu have regained their status as an integral unit of the territory of the Republic of China.[4]

[1] Ely Maurer, "Legal Problems Regarding Formosa and the Offshore Islands," *Department of State Bulletin*, Vol. 39, No. 1017, December 1958, p. 1009.

[2] Quincy Wright, "The Chinese Recognition Problem," *The American Journal of International Law*, Vol. 49, No. 2, April 1955, p. 324.

[3] *Ibid.*, p. 329.

[1] Chiang Kai-shek, *op. cit.*, p. 3.

In the opinion of the Nationalist Government, its presence on Formosa and its right to remain there cannot be questioned. To the Chinese, the island has always been considered a part of China despite the fact that foreign states consider its status as undetermined.[1]

Legitimacy of Nationalist China's Claims

The Republic of China has based its claims to title of Formosa on several legal but controversial issues. The first of these issues is its claim that the provisions of the Cairo Declaration have given it the legal right to title of the island. In discussing his Government's views on the subject, President Chiang Kai-shek observed:

> Some people deny the validity of the Cairo Declaration in order to justify their distorted views about the status of Taiwan.[2]

The Republic of China contends that the act to incorporate Formosa as a territory of China was taken and became legal by virtue of the Cairo Declaration. This view is not shared by some jurists, such as D. P. O'Connell. Dr. O'Connell in commenting on the subject stated:

> There is... little evidence that the decisions arrived at in Cairo and to which Japan acceded have any legal characteristics... The only alternative, then, is to regard China as in military occupation of Japanese territory.[3]

The legal effect of declarations depends on the terminology used in the document and on the intention of the signatories. The Cairo Declaration appears to be a statement of purpose rather than an international agreement from which would flow international rights and obligations.

A second claim advanced by the Republic of China relative to sovereignty over Formosa is its abrogation of the Treaty of Shimonoseki. In a news conference on October 16, 1959, a spokesman for the Ministry of Foreign affairs commented:

> When China declared war on Japan on December 9, 1941, she also declared that "All treaties, conventions, agreements, and contracts concerning the relations between China and Japan, are and remain null and void." The Treaty of Shimonoseki was one of such treaties.[4]

International lawyers are not in agreement on the validity of unilateral abrogation of treaties. Some writers, such as Professor Oppen-

[1] John Gange, "Chinese Decisions Discussed," New York *Times*, February 1, 1955, Col. 6, p. 28.
[2] Chiang Kai-shek, *op. cit.*, p. 3.
[3] D. P. O'Connell, *op. cit.*, p. 427.
[4] Republic of China, Government Information Office, News Conference, October 16, 1959, Text of an answer to a "Question From the Press by the Spokesman of the Ministry of Foreign Affairs," p. 1.

heim, contend that treaties which are signed under duress are, in some instances, not valid. In this connection, Oppenheim observed:

It has been rightly suggested with regard to the abrogation of treaties as the result of war, that it may be improper for courts to recognize, in a way benefitting the aggressor state, the automatic termination of treaties in consequence of a war launched by him. It follows also that a peace treaty imposed by the victorious aggressor has no legal validity, notwithstanding the rule that international law disregards the vitiating effect of duress.[1]

If this position is to be accepted, then it would appear that the claims of the Nationalists have some validity. There is no question that the Japanese Government was the aggressor in the Sino-Japanese war and that Formosa was its prime objective. It should be observed, however, that not all jurists share Professor Oppenheim's views. The general practice in international law is that treaties of cession signed as a result of war are valid. In commenting on the subject, Professor Fenwick observed:

Treaties of cession are considered "Executed" treaties, dealing with single acts which are to be performed forthwith and which when performed dispose of the matter once and for all.[2]

The arguments presented by Professor Oppenheim and by the Republic of China are based on moral, rather than legal grounds. Although such acts should not be condoned by the law of nations, the fact remains that no corrective measures have been established to render such cessions invalid.

Transfer of Title through a Treaty of Cession

It is entirely possible for Formosa to be ceded to the Republic of China by a treaty of cession with the Allied Powers. The treaty could be effected by the signatories of the Cairo Declaration and the Potsdam Proclamation. However, since Great Britain and the Soviet Union do not recognize the Nationalist Government, it appears that the United States, if it so chose, could effect such a treaty with the Nationalist Government. The United States could justify its action based on the following reasons: (1) The island has been considered derelict as a result of the San Francisco Peace Treaty; (2) the United States was mainly responsible for Japan's defeat; (3) of the Allied Powers that signed the Cairo Declaration, the United States alone continues to recognize the Republic of China; (4) the United States is a signatory of the San Francisco Peace Treaty.

[1] L. Oppenheim, Vol. 2, *op. cit.*, p. 219.
[2] Fenwick, *op. cit.*, p. 331.

Consequently, the Republic of China has the legal right to enter into a treaty of cession with the United States because the Republic of China is in *de facto* control of the territory and is considered one of the Allied Powers that was at war with Japan. Furthermore, since the Allied Powers have failed to act collectively, it appears that the United States and the Nationalist Government are no longer restrained from concluding the treaty of cession.

Title through Prescription

It does not appear likely that the question of Formosa's status will be settled by peaceful means. Both claimants have sworn to eliminate the other if and when the opportunity presents itself. In addition, both the Nationalist Chinese and the Communist Chinese have refused all offers of mediation in the dispute and have consistently rejected all solutions proposed by the Allied Powers and the United Nations.

The arguments advanced by Taipei and Peiping relative to conquest and annexation, abrogation of the Treaty of Shimonoseki, the Cairo Declaration, and the Treaty of San Francisco have been found to be either questionable or legally invalid. It appears, however, "that the only argument which could be profitably adduced in favor of Nationalist China is that of *de facto* occupation.[1] The principle of prescription cannot be applied to the claims of Red China since that government has never held legal title to the island, nor has it ever exercised *de facto* control over the territory.

The Republic of China did not consider the occupation of Formosa as a temporary measure. It immediately re-established its sovereignty over the island by proclaiming it a province of China soon after assuming administration of the territory. This action was not objected to by the Allied Powers. However, it was generally assumed that *de jure* sovereignty remained with Japan.

The dereliction of Formosa as a result of the Treaty of San Francisco relieved Japan of *de jure* sovereignty of the island. At that time, the Allied Powers did not collectively or individually exercise condominium over the territory. It follows that since the Republic of China had been in continuous *de facto* control of the territory since 1945, that *de jure* sovereignty could have passed to that government.

In accordance with the practice of international law, title to territory may be acquired by prescription through uninterrupted and un-

[1] J. P. Jain, "The Legal Status of Formosa," *The American Journal of International Law*, Vol. 57, January 1963, p. 44-45.

contested possession for a sufficient length of time.[1] In discussing the subject, Professor Oppenheim is of the opinion that no general rule can be laid down as regards the length of the time which is necessary to create a title by prescription. According to Oppenheim, prescription in international law may be defined as:

the acquisition of sovereignty over a territory through continuous and undisturbed exercise of sovereignty over it during such a period as is necessary to create under the influence of historical development the general conviction that the present condition of things is in conformity with international order.[2]

Professor Hyde, though agreeing with the opinions of Professors Wilson and Oppenheim, has qualified the definition of prescription by declaring that:

It must be clear that it is uninterrupted and undisturbed possession implying full acquiescence on the part of the foreign and dispossessed claimant, which in theory serves to rob it of its rights and to lodge them in the actual occupant.[3]

It should be observed that there can be little doubt about Japan's complete acquiescence in its renunciation of title to Formosa and of the Nationalist Government's continuous *de facto* control of the territory since the end of World War II. The application of the principle of prescription can be seen in *The Island of Palmas Case* (*United States and The Netherlands*), decided by the Permanent Court of Arbitration in 1928, and in the case of *Rhode Island versus State of Massachusetts*, decided in the United States Supreme Court in 1846.

In the Island of Palmas case, the decision was delivered by Max Huber, acting as arbitrator for the Permanent Court of Arbitration. In deciding against the United States' claim to title of the island based on the principle of contiguity, Justice Huber found that the Netherlands had possessed and exercised rights of sovereignty over the island since 1677. Moreover, the arbitrator could find no evidence that would establish any act of display of sovereignty over the island by any power other than the Netherlands. In view of his findings, Justice Huber declared:

The Netherlands' title of sovereignty acquired by continuous and peaceful display of state authority during a long period of time... therefore holds good.[4]

In the boundary dispute between Rhode Island and Massachusetts, the Supreme Court applied the principle of prescription to settle the

[1] Wilson, *op. cit.*, p. 79.
[2] Oppenheim, Vol. 1, *op. cit.*, p. 576.
[3] Hyde, Vol. 1, *op. cit.*, p. 388.
[4] Bishop, *op. cit.* p. 265-271.

controversy. Mr. Justice McLean, in delivering the opinion of the Court, found that the commissioners of both states had agreed to a boundary line, however in error, in 1710-1711. Furthermore, he found that Massachusetts took possession of the territory and steadily maintained such possession since that time. Therefore, by applying the rule of continuous and undisturbed exercise of sovereignty over the disputed territory, Justice McLean declared:

> For the security of right, whether of states or individuals, long possession under a claim of title is protected.[1]

It is evident from what has been discussed thus far that international law has long recognized as valid the principle of prescription as a mode of acquiring territory. That this position is shared by present day jurists can be seen in the comments of Professor Schwarzenberger in his discussion of the acquisition of territory. It is the opinion of Professor Schwarzenberger that:

> The actual exercise of territorial jurisdiction tends to create a presumption in favor of the right to exercise such jurisdiction. If such *de facto* exercise of jurisdiction is continuous and, in relation to other states, peaceful, that is to say, not contested, such a position is as good as title.[2]

Except for the claims of Red China, whose own status is questionable, it can be said that the occupation of Formosa by the Nationalist Government has been undisturbed. In addition, this *de facto* exercise of governmental authority has been continuous for nineteen years. The possession of Formosa by the Nationalist Government has been steadily maintained by an assertion of right. It follows that if the principle of prescription, as interpreted and applied within the framework of international law, is to be accepted in the case of China, then there can be no lawyer's doubts as to the legitimacy of Nationalist China's title to Formosa.

[1] Fenwick, *Cases on International Law*, p. 484-488.

[2] Georg Schwarzenberger, "Title to Territory: Response to a Challenge," *The American Journal of International Law*, Vol. 51, 1957, p. 312.

VIII. PRESENT STATUS OF FORMOSA

The present military and political conditions in China render it unlikely that the legal status of Formosa will be resolved by applying the principles of international law. There have been several significant factors that have precluded the possibility of a peaceful solution to the problem. Foremost is the inflexible positions taken by Taipei and Peiping in the controversy. Each entity has claimed title to the island on the basis that it is the rightful government of China. As a logical consequence, the rival entities have adamantly refused to recognize the existence of the other. Under such conditions, negotiations of any kind are not possible. The second factor is that the United Nations is closely linked to the legal status of Formosa. As a matter of fact, neither the Nationalist Government nor the Chinese Communists recognize the existence of a problem concerning the status of Formosa. According to Taipei and Peiping, the island is an integral part of China. A third factor that has prevented a peaceful solution to the problem has been the reluctance of the Allied Powers to carry out the commitments made to the Republic of China in the Cairo Declaration.

In examining the legal aspects of the Formosan question, it was observed that the island has been in the possession of the Nationalist Government since 1945. Since that time, the Nationalist Government has exercised effective control over the territory and is accepted by many overseas Chinese as the Government of China. Furthermore, the government is currently recognized by a majority of the member states of the United Nations as the legal government of the Republic of China. However, its claims to sovereignty over Formosa are disputed by the Allied Powers on the grounds that the legal status of the island is as yet undetermined. In this instance, the Allied Powers dispute China's claim that title passed from Japan to China as a result of the Cairo Declaration, the unilateral abrogation of the Treaty of Shimonoseki, or the terms of the Treaty of San Francisco.

The Republic of China's claim to the island has also been challenged by the Formosan nationalists on the grounds that Formosans are not Chinese. In using the ethnic argument as a basis for their claims, the Formosans have requested either complete independence from

China or the imposition of a United Nations trusteeship on the island.

The claims of the Formosan nationalists appear questionable for several reasons. First, an examination of the island's history leaves little doubt that Formosa is both ethnically and historically Chinese. Second, the question of independence for the Formosans is not related to the legal status of the island. This island's status is a matter between the Republic of China and the Allied Powers. The Formosans, as subjects of the Republic of China, are not international persons. As such, they are subject to the laws of that Government and cannot legally request the United Nations to take action in their behalf. Consequently, the question of independence is an internal matter between the Formosan nationalists and the Nationalist Government.

It is the contention of the Republic of China that title to Formosa passed to China at the time of Japan's acceptance of the terms of surrender. Under these terms, Japan agreed to accept the provisions of the Cairo Declaration. It should be observed that international law is not clear about the legal character of declarations. The general practice in international law is that statements of common policy and principles are binding only upon the signatories. However, even in such instances, it is not clear whether a contractual obligation has been effected between the signatories.

In most instances the legal character of a declaration depends to a large extent upon the precision of the language used in the agreement. Such declarations are considered binding upon the signatories. However, international law is not clear about the legal effect of such agreements on states that were not signatories to the transaction.

It is evident from the discussion thus far that the legal character of the Cairo Declaration and the Potsdam Proclamation appears to be questionable. Justification for this argument is based on the fact that these transactions were not couched in legal terms. From the standpoint of international law, the Cairo and Potsdam transactions appear to be statements of purpose concerning the disposition of Japanese territories after the war that were agreed upon by the Allied Powers. Hence, if the accepted practice of international law is to be applied in connection with these agreements, title to Formosa did not pass to China. Under such conditions, the claims of the Nationalist Government do not appear to be legally valid. It should be observed, however, that the Allied Powers were morally bound to carry out the provisions of the Cairo and Potsdam transactions.

The positions taken by the Allied Powers on the status of Formosa appear to be based on political considerations rather than on the legal principles of international law.

The Soviet Union contends that the entire Chinese question is an internal affair of China. Any question concerning the status of Formosa is not the concern of the United Nations. According to the Russian point of view, the island is Chinese territory and the Peiping regime has the right to liberate it by force.

Russia's position on the China question has been influenced by its relations with the Chinese Communists and by its implication in the revolutionary conspiracy. Russia was unquestionably guilty of violating international law as well as the Sino-Russian Treaty of 1945. Its position, therefore, is not based on the principles of international law, but on the Leninist principle of world revolution. It is significant that the recent ideological split between the two Communist powers has made no change in the Russian position on the China question.

The British hold that the status of Formosa is as yet undetermined and that the island is under the condominium of the Allied Powers. Furthermore, the conflict between the rival Chinese factions cannot be considered a civil war in the accepted definition of the term. The conflict, according to the British, is international in scope. Pursuing this line of argument, the British contend that the Formosan problem should be settled by negotiation rather than by force.

Both the Nationalist Chinese and the Communist Chinese have rejected the British view on the grounds that Formosa is Chinese territory. However, the British contention that the sovereignty of the island did not pass from Japan to China as a result of the San Francisco Treaty appears to be valid. In this instance, neither of the claimant entities were signatories to that transaction nor did the Japanese Government cede the island to them.

The British theory of condominium appears to be questionable for several reasons. First, there is the question of the dereliction of the territory at the time of Japan's renunciation. If the island had not been occupied by a sovereign government or if it had remained unclaimed, the British theory would have had some substance in law. However, Nationalist China both occupied and claimed title to the island long before Japan renounced its sovereignty. In the second instance, the Allied Powers did not choose to exercise the alleged right of condominium at the time of Japan's renunciation. In addition, it is not clear how title of the territory could pass from Japan to the co-signatories of the San Francisco Treaty. It should be observed that Japan did not renounce title to the territory in favor of the co-signatories, nor did the Treaty provide for a condominium by those powers. Consequently, any action taken by the co-signatories to the treaty to exercise condominiun or to determine the status of Formosa would not be legally justified.

Prior to the outbreak of the Korean war, the United States held that Formosa was an integral part of China. However, after the Communist Chinese entered the conflict, the American position on the island's status suffered a reversal. In a policy statement on the China question, the spokesman for the United States declared that the legal status of the island was yet to be determined. This change of policy was influenced by the necessity for the President to send the Seventh Fleet into the Formosan Strait without being accused of intervening in the domestic affairs of China.

In justifying its actions, the United States held that the China question was one of international concern. Therefore, in order to maintain peace in Asia, the Seventh Fleet would prevent either of the claimant entities from attacking the other.

Here again it is evident that the American action was based on military and political considerations rather than on legal principles. The San Francisco Treaty had not been signed at the time the American change in policy took place; therefore, it is not clear on what legal principle the United States based its decision. A few years earlier, the United States did not object to Nationalist China's occupation of Formosa and the apparent integration of the island into Chinese territory. Yet, the American attitude changed when the situation in Asia worsened. It is evident that the *de jure* status of Formosa could not have been affected by the Korean conflict or by the Chinese Communist threat of invasion. In view of these facts, the American change of policy appears questionable.

The two-China concept proposed by Great Britain and India as a solution to the Formosan problem has been rejected by Taipei and Peiping as unrealistic. If the British proposal were to be accepted, one of the claimant entities would have to sever all ties with China and assume a new international personality. However, neither the Nationalist Government nor the Peiping regime has indicated any desire to relinquish its sovereignty over any portion of Chinese territory. It appears that both governments are correct in rejecting the two-China concept. International law does not recognize the concept of two governments representing the same people. It follows that only one of the claimants can rightfully represent the Chinese people. It is apparent, therefore, that the China question may not be amenable to peaceful solution. Moreover, even if a political solution were possible, the legal status of the island would not be settled.

The Peiping regime holds that title of Formosa has passed to China as a result of conquest and annexation. The Chinese Communist argument is based on the Republic of China's unilateral abrogation of the Treaty of Shimonoseki. The argument advanced by Peiping appears to be questionable for several reasons. In the first instance, international law does not recognize the unilateral abrogation of treaties involving the cession of territory. The second reason is the fact that the Communist Chinese have never exercised *de facto* control over the territory.

More important, however, is the fact that the legal status of the Peiping regime itself is in question. There can be no denial of the *de facto* existence of the Peiping regime. It is a government and it exercises effective authority over the Chinese mainland. Normally in accordance with the declaratory or *de facto* doctrine of international law, third states would not long withhold recognition of states that have come to power as a result of revolution. However, in the case of Communist China, there appear to be extenuating circumstances.

The Republic of China was the first Government to be subverted and overthrown as a result of the Communist revolutionary conspiracy. The goal of these revolutionary governments is not to improve the lot of their people, but to spread Communism throughout the world. The legitimacy of such governments, therefore, cannot and should not be determined by the present *de facto* doctrine of international law. The legitimacy of governments born of the Communist revolutionary conspiracy should be decided by the International Court of Justice. From such legal decisions there could evolve a new and more meaningful doctrine of recognition which would replace the present doctrine of *de facto* recognition, a doctrine which is sometimes ineffective and meaningless.

It follows that until the legitimacy of Red China is legally determined, its claims to sovereignty over all of China, much less over Formosa, cannot be a matter for serious consideration by the Allied Powers.

An examination of the claims of the Republic of China indicates that its arguments for title to Formosa based on the Cairo Declaration and the abrogation of the Treaty of Shimonoseki are questionable.

Formosa's dereliction as a result of the Treaty of San Francisco has made it possible for the island to be ceded to the Republic of China by the signatories to the Potsdam Proclamation. In this instance, however, it does not appear possible that Great Britain or Russia could enter into such a transaction because neither of these powers now recognize the Nationalist Government. Therefore, it remains for the United States as the only signatory which continues to recognize Nationalist China, to examine the legal aspect of such a transaction. If a cession is legally possible, it would then be incumbent upon the United States to carry out the obligations it assumed under the terms of the Potsdam Proclamation, even though they may be based on moral considerations.

The only argument which has been advanced by the Nationalist Government and which appears to validate its claim to Formosa is that of prescription. International law generally recognizes prescription as one of the modes in which sovereignty over a territory is transferred from one state to another. At the time Formosa became derelict, the Republic of China had been in continuous and undisturbed *de facto* control of the territory since the close of World War II. In addition, at the time of dereliction, the Allied Powers did not choose to exercise the right of condominium over the territory. Under these circumstances, it is evident that the principle of prescription is applicable in the case of Formosa. The principle of prescription fully supports and validates the Republic of China's claim to the territory; there can be no lawyer's doubts about that. It can be said, therefore, that title to Formosa passed from Japan to the Republic of China at the time of dereliction.

BIBLIOGRAPHY

OFFICIAL DOCUMENTS - REPUBLIC OF CHINA

The Constitution of the Republic of China, Promulgated by the National Government January 1, 1947; Effective from December 25, 1947, Taipei, Taiwan.

Treaty of Peace Between the Republic of China and Japan, Taipei, Taiwan, April 29, 1952.

OFFICIAL DOCUMENTS - UNITED NATIONS

General Assembly, *Official Records*, First Committee, 338th Meeting September 25, 1949; Fourth Session, 230 Plenary Meeting, September 29, 1949; Fifth Session, 284 Plenary Meeting, September 26, 1950; 286 Plenary Meeting, September 27, 1950; Sixteenth Session, 1072 Plenary Meeting, September 27, 1950; Sixth Session, 341 Plenary Meeting, November 13, 1951; Sixth Session, 342 Plenary Meeting, November 13, 1951; Tenth Session, 516 Plenary Meeting, September 20, 1955; 578 Plenary Meeting, November 15, 1956; Eleventh Session, 658 Plenary Meeting, February 21, 1957; Thirteenth Session, 752 Plenary Meeting, September 22, 1958; Thirteenth Session, 774 Plenary Meeting, October 7, 1958; Sixteenth Session, 1068 Plenary Meeting December 1, 1961; Plenary Meeting, October 30, 1962; Nineteenth Session, (A/PV 1295), December 8, 1964.

Security Council, *Official Records*, 490th Meeting, August 25, 1960.

OFFICIAL DOCUMENTS - UNITED STATES

Department of State, *Bulletins*:

Bulletin No. 324, Publication No. 2384, Vol. 13, 1945; Bulletin No. 550, Vol. 22; Bulletin No. 657, Vol. 26, January 28, 1952; Bulletin No. 1005, Vol. 39, 1956; Bulletin No. 1017, Vol. 39, December 22, 1958; Bulletin No. 1006, Vol. 39, 1958; Bulletin No. 1017, Vol. 39, 1959; Bulletin No. 1272, Vol. XLIX, November 11, 1963.

Department of State, *Publications*:

Publication No. 7187, 1943: Publication No. 2504, Executive Agreement Series 493, 1946; Publication No. 4613, TIAS 2490, October, 1954; Publication No. 6199, 1955; Publication No. 6705, Far Eastern Series 76, 1958; Publication No. 6844, Far Eastern Series 81, October, 1959; The Conlon Report, Study No. 5, September, 1960; Publication No. 7015, Vol. 1, 1960.

BOOKS

Ballantine, Joseph W., *Formosa, A Problem For United States Foreign Policy*, Menasha, Wisconsin, 1952.

Bate, H. Maclear, *Report From Formosa*, New York, 1952.

Bishop, William W., Jr., *International Law, Cases and Materials*, Boston, 1953.
Brierly, J. L., *The Law of Nations*, Oxford, 1961.
Brown, Benjamin H., Chinese Representation: *A Case Study in United Nations Political Affairs*, New York, 1955.
Chang, Carson, *The Third Force In China*, New York, 1952.
Chen, Ti-Chiang, *The International Law of Recognition*, New York, 1951.
Cheng, Tien-fong, *A History of Sino-Soviet Relations*, Washington, D.C., 1957.
Chiang Kai-shek, *Soviet Russia In China*, New York, 1957.
China Yearbook, 1957-1958; 1960-1961, (compiled by China Yearbook Editorial Board), Taipei, Taiwan, 1958; 1961.
Chow, Ching-wen, *Ten Years of Storm*, New York, 1960.
Dallin, David J., *Soviet Russia and The Far East*, New Haven, 1948.
Dallin, David, J., *The Rise of Soviet Russia In Asia*, New Haven, 1949.
Davidson, James, William, *The Island of Formosa, Past and Present*, New York, 1903.
Elegant, Robert S., *China's Red Masters*, New York, 1951.
Esch, P. A. M. Van der, *Prelude to War*, The Hague, 1951.
Fenwick, Charles G., *Cases On International Law*, Chicago, 1951.
Fenwick, Charles G., *International Law*, New York, 1952.
Gentili, Alberico, *De Jure Belli, Libri Tres*, Vol. 2 (The translation of the edition of 1612, by John Rolfe) Oxford, 1933.
Grotius, Hugo, *De Jure Belli Ac Pacis*, Libri Tres, Vol. 2, (The translation of Book III by Francis W. Kelsy), Oxford, 1925.
Hyde, Charles Cheney, *International Law, Chiefly as Interpreted and Applied by the United States*, Vols. 1 and 3, Boston, 1951.
Lauterpacht, Hersch, "The Problem of Nonrecognition," in *Legal Problems in the Far Eastern Conflict*, by Quincy Wright, New York, 1941.
Lauterpacht, Hersch, *Recognition In International Law*, Cambridge, 1948.
Mao Tse-tung, *The Selected Works of Mao Tse-tung*, Vols. 1 and 3, New York, 1955.
Moore, John Basset, *A Digest of International Law*, Vol. 1, Washington, D.C., 1906.
North, Robert C., *Moscow and Chinese Communists*, California, 1953.
Oppenheim, L., *International Law, A Treatise*, Vols. 1 and 2, (ed. by H. Lauterpacht), London, 1955.
Pan Wei-tung, *The Chinese Constitution*, Washington, D.C., 1946.
Pufendorf, Samuel, *De Jure Naturae Et Gentium, Liber Octo.*, Vol. 2, (translation of the edition of 1688 by C. H. Oldfather and W. A. Oldfather), Oxford, 1934.
Rutter, Owen, *Through Formosa, An Account of Japan's Island Colony*, London, 1923.
Schwarzenberger, Georg, *A Manual of International Law*, Vol. 1, New York, 1960.
Starke, Joseph G., *An Introduction Into International Law*, London. 1947.
Takekoshi, Yosaburo, *Japanese Rule in Formosa*, (translation by George Braithwaite), London, 1907.
Tung, William L., *China and Some Phases of International Law*, London, New York, 1940.
Tung, William L., *Cases and Other Readings on International Law*, Shanghai, 1940.
Tung, William L., *The Political Institutions of Modern China*, The Hague, 1964.
Vattel, E. de, *The Law of Nations*, (translation of the edition of 1758 by Charles G. Fenwick), Vol. 3, Washington, D.C., 1916.

Von Schuschnigg, Kurt, *International Law, An Introduction to the Law of Peace*, Milwaukee, 1959.

Whiting, Allen S., *Soviet Policies In China, 1917-1924*, New York, 1957.

Wilbur, Martin C., and How, Julie Lien-ying, (editors), *Documents on Communism, Nationalism and Soviet Advisers in China, 1918-1927*, New York, 1956.

Wilson, George Grafton, *International Law*, ninth edition, New York, 1935.

Wolf, Christian, *The Classics of International Law*, (ed. James Brown Scott; translated by Joseph H. Drake), London, 1934.

Zouche, Richard, *An Exposition of Fecial Law and Procedure of Law Between Nations and Laws Concerning the Same*, Vol. II (translation by James L. Brierly; edited by James B. Scott), Washington, D.C. 1911.

PAMPHLETS

Giap, General Vo Nguyen, *People's War, People's Army*, Pamphlet AD 292744, Arlington, Virginia, 1955.

Liao, Joshua, *Formosa Speaks*, Hong Kong, 1950.

Lin Yutang, *An Analysis of the Conlon Report: Its Fallacies and Contradictions as Viewed by Asians*, (Unpublished Paper in Mimeograph Form), New York, January 1960.

Sih, Dr. Paul K. T., *Two Chinas: Fact and Myth*, Washington, D.C., 1962.

ARTICLES (Periodicals)

Bowles, Chester, "The China Problem Reconsidered," *Foreign Affairs*, Vol. 38, (April 1960), p. 479-482.

Chao Yin-ming, "The Sovereignty of Taiwan From the Viewpoint of International Law; *Political Review*, Taipei, Formosa, Vol. 13, No. 12, (Reprinted in the Central Daily News, Taipei, March 5, 1965.).

Cooper, Colonel Wade H., "International Law and Current Problems in the Far East," *Proceedings of the American Society of International Law*, Washington D.C. (April, 1955), p. 103-107.

Dean, Arthur H., "United States Foreign Policy and Formosa," *Foreign Affairs*, Vol. 33, (April, 1955), p. 3072.

Dean, Arthur, H., "International Law and Current Problems in the Far East," *Proceedings of the American Society of International Law*, Washington, D.C., April 1955), p. 81-95.

Dillard, Hardy Cross, "The Problem of Recognition," *The Yale Review*, Vol. 64, (February 1954), p. 128-183.

Godber, J. B., M.P., "Chinese Representation in the United Nations," *British Information Services*, T-56, (December 12, 1960), p. 1-3.

Harvey, Richard, "The Legal Status of Formosa," *World Affairs Quarterly*, Vol. 30, (1959-60), p. 134-153.

Hishida, Seiji, "Formosa, Japan's First Colony," *Political Science Quarterly*, Vol. 22, (January 1940), p. 264-269.

Hornbeck, Stanley K., "International Problems in the Far East," *Proceedings of the American Society of International Law*, (April 1955), p. 106-108.

Hoyt, Edwin C., "The United States Reaction to the Korean Attack," *American Journal of International Law*, Vol. 55 (January 1961), p. 60-71.

Hsiu, Chuan-wu, "Important Documents Concerning the Question of Taiwan:

United States Armed Aggression Against Taiwan," *Foreign Language Press*, (February 1955), p. 21-23.
Hu, Shih, "China, In Stalin's Grand Strategy," *Foreign Affairs*, (October 1950), p. 14-37.
Jain, J. P., "The Legal Status of Formosa," *American Journal of International Law*, Vol. 57, No. 1, (January 1963), p. 16-57.
Johnson, D. H. N., "Public International Law," *The British Year Book of International Law*, Vol. 29, (1952), p. 464-469.
Khan, Mohammed Samin, "Legal Aspects of the Problem of China's Representation in the United Nations," *Pakistan Horizon*, Vol. 10, No. 3, (September 1957), p. 138-144.
Kleinwachter, George, "The History of Formosa Under the Chinese Nationalist Government," *China Review*, Hong Kong (1884), p. 383-388.
Lauterpacht, E., "Effect of Cairo and Potsdam Declarations 1943- and 1946," *The International and Comparative Law Quarterly*, Vol. 8 part 1, (January 1959), p. 182-189.
Lauterpacht, E., "Sovereignty In Suspense," *The International and Comparative Law Quarterly*, Vol. 5, Part 3, (July 1956), p. 411-416.
Li, Thian-hok, "The China Impasse," *Foreign Affairs*, Vol. 36, No. 3, (April 1958), p. 441-453.
Morse, Hosea B., " A Short Lived Republic," *New China Review*, Vol. 1, Hong Kong, (1919), p. 30-39.
O'Connell, D. P., "Legal Aspects of the Peace Treaty with Japan," *The British Year Book of International Law*, Vol. 39, (1953), London, p. 419-428.
O'Connell, D. P., "The Status of Formosa and The Chinese Recognition Problem, *The American Journal of International Law*, Vol. 50, No. 2, (April 1956), p. 403-409.
Padeford, Norman J., "The International Non-Intervention Agreement and the Spanish Civil War," *The American Journal of International Law*, Vol. 31, (1937), p. 587-608.
Peoples Daily, (Jenmin Jihpao), "Peiping Opposes one China one Taiwan Plot," (May 12, 1964), *Chinese News Service*, B. No. 3, (May 25, 1964), p. 1-2.
Phillips, Claude S., "The International Legal Status of Formosa," *Western Political Quarterly*, Vol. 10, (1957), p. 267-289.
Schwarzenberger, Georg, "Title to Territory: Response to a Challenge," *The American Journal of International Law*, Vol. 51, (1957), p. 311-314.
Spokesman, Ministry of Foreign Affairs (News Conference of October 16, 1959), Government Information Office, Taipei, p. 2-3.
Wright, Quincy, "The Chinese Recognition Problem," *The American Journal of International Law*, Vol. 49, No. 2, (April 1955), p. 318-327.

ARTICLES (Newspaper)

Bodde, Derek, "Interference In Civil War Seen," *New York Times*, February 3, 1955, p. 27, Col. 6.
Chandler, Bronson W., "New Status For Formosa," *New York Times*, February 1, 1955, p. 28, Col. 7.
Chen, I-te, "Formosa's Independence," *New York Times*, December 24, 1964, p. 26, Col. 4.
Editorial, "Peiping Stresses Army's Readiness," *New York Times*, October 31, 1958, p. 10, Col. 7.

Gange, John, "Chinese Decision Discussed," *New York Times*, February 1, 1955, p. 28, Col. 6.
Grew, Joseph, "Support of Taiwan Urged," *New York Times*, October 31, 1958, Section 4, p. 8, Col. 5.
Kotelawala, Sir John, "Colombian Plan," *New York Times*, April 22, 1955, p. 2, Col. 4.
Li Tze-chung, "Against Formosa Plebiscite," *New York Times*, December 10, 1964, p. 28, Col. 6.
Nakae, Y., First Secretary, Permanent Mission of Japan to the United Nations, *Letter dated February* 19, 1963, New York, p. 1.
Schwarzenberger, Georg, "Letter to the Editor," *The Times*, London, February 2, 1955, p. 6, Col. 4.
Stone, N. I., "Policy on Red China," *New York Times*, February 3, 1955, p. 22, Col. 6.
Vincent, John Carter, "Two China Plan Opposed," *New York Times*, December 4, 1961, Section 4, p. 8, Col. 5.

INDEX

GPSR Compliance

The European Union's (EU) General Product Safety Regulation (GPSR) is a set of rules that requires consumer products to be safe and our obligations to ensure this.

If you have any concerns about our products, you can contact us on ProductSafety@springernature.com

In case Publisher is established outside the EU, the EU authorized representative is:

Springer Nature Customer Service Center GmbH
Europaplatz 3
69115 Heidelberg, Germany

Batch number: 10830943

Printed by Printforce, the Netherlands